U0136279

名家水墨

蕭海春

Masterpieces of Ink Painting

Xiao Haichun

目錄 CONTENTS

序

蕭海春先生，出生於一九四四年，江西豐城人，於一九六一年入上海工藝美術學校，學習傳統繪畫和雕刻，曾受著王康樂及顧飛指導。一九六四年畢業後進入上海雕刻廠，從事專業設計工作，同時並開始中國畫創作。自一九六七年起，蕭海春曾赴各地寫生，足跡步遍中國各地之名山大水，首先赴雁蕩山，次年赴江西井岡山，觀五指峰，也曾赴湖南、北上西安、銅川至延安。後又入四川長江三峽寫生，一九七八年之後他又赴雲貴高原，又赴西北寫生，考察石刻。九〇年代後，中國與國際交流漸頻，蕭海春先後在北京、上海、新加坡、香港、台北舉辦展覽，受大眾喜愛，作品廣爲各地收藏家鍾愛典藏。

蕭海春的筆墨不脫傳統，許多畫中可看出他參照古畫的水墨精神，他所仿的古畫中，不論是董源、范寬、倪瓚、王原祁、龔賢，都顯出他筆墨的厚實功力，不爲傳統所拘泥，賦予山水畫新的語言及意境。蕭海春的山水畫，大量使用綿密的點或線，他的用筆密密麻麻的，反覆渲染，一張畫經過七、八次甚至數十次的點染，一層層的加疊上去，用色上，蕭的畫很黑，但是在黑的墨色中，包涵了許多的層次。他以此建構出一幅幅山川奇境。在畫面上，他追求完整、謹嚴、細密的筆墨，在構圖上以塊壘結構及細密的點法爲特徵，因此就算是小幅作品，畫面上也依然是層嶂疊罩，展示出同樣的氣勢及擴張力。

收藏家張平沼先生雖從事企業數十年，但對書畫有所愛好，積累圖書滿室，然猶書畫不釋手，談論書畫，亦不陌生。此次籌辦名家水墨展，承張先生提供蕭海春作品一〇三幅，出版專集圖錄，特此申謝。

國立歷史博物館　前館長

黃光男　謹識

PREFACE

Xiao Haichun was born in 1944 in Fengcheng, Jiangxi province. In 1961, he entered the Art and Craft School of Shanghai and studied traditional painting and sculpture from Wang Kangle and Gu Fei. He graduated in 1964 and began to work in Shanghai Sculpture Factory as a designer. In 1967, he began to travel extensively to a variety of different destinations in China. He has climbed many mountains, leaving his footsteps in Mount Yandang, and Mount Jinggang in Jiangxi. He's also been to Hunan, Xian, Tongchuan, Yanan and Sichuan. In 1978 he visited Yungui Plateau and the Buddhist caves of northwest China, where he made many copies of cave wall paintings. In the 1990s, with the increasing contacts between China and other countries, Xiao's works were shown in Beijing, Shanghai, Singapore, Hong Kong and Taipei. His works were well received by many people and many of his works were acquired by private collectors.

Xiao Haichun expressed great respect for tradition. In line with a great tradition within Chinese art, he imitates the works of old masters including Dong Yuan, Fan Kuan, Wang Yuanqi, and Kong Xian. Many excellent paintings of this kind reveal his studying carefully of traditional brushwork and techniques. He used many short, choppy strokes, to very short, curving strokes, piled up in some areas to obtain great density. In his pictures, the play of tones of the dry ink is constantly varied. He often applies many layers of ink washes, which builds a complicated effect of tonal variations. His aim is to create a strong, powerful and restless composition. The effort shows even in his small pictures.

Very special thanks go to Mr. Zhang Pingzhao for providing a selection of paintings to show in the exhibition as well as for his assistance in the publication of the catalogue. Mr. Zhang is well known for his management skills and his passion for art. He is a knowledgeable art collector who spent years studying traditional ink paintings. The exhibition will feature 103 paintings by Xiao Haichun from Zhang's collection.

Dr. Kuang-nan Huang, Former Director
National Museum of History

蕭海春小傳

文◎蕭海春

一九四四年三月，我出生于上海浦江之濱。祖籍江西。先父母皆不識字，唯賴勤儉，勉持家計，謀生海上。育有三子五女，以我爲長。

幼時，我不善言辭，而性喜塗抹，且癖性落根。雖時遭師長呵斥，卻無怨不悔。如此一發迄今不可收也。

稍長，求學於上海工藝美校，專攻玉雕。既爲唯一之正規美術訓練，亦是我最高學歷。

理玉雖爲小技，然惠我良多，受用終生。琢磨切磋，其要在智勇忍耐。亦即琢璞爲玉，須有隨機之智，走險之勇，繁複之忍，時日之耐。所謂廢寢忘食不知東方既白而意猶未盡。如此經久歷練，得與失，遇而化，唯投入其中者能感而悟。

既而志於畫。畫之爲畫，自有其道。古人云：“五日一石，十日一水”。乃爲至理名言，其要旨在一“慢”字。“慢”之義有三：一曰平心靜氣，一曰切磋揣摩，一曰循進漸變。得此要義，則既不至於菲薄傳統，又不至於杜撰新篇。水到渠成，絕活始出。故時有新舊，畫分優劣，其中意蘊，恰如池水之冷暖唯有魚自知。

我欽慕石濤與石溪，額齋室名曰“二石齋”；轉而服膺八大山人，遂額齋室名曰“抱雪齋”；又醉心董玄宰，更齋室名曰“煙雲堂”。於此更疊之中，或可略知吾意趣之所在。

我性好靜，拗且迂。不喜交際，卻不乏至交。喜美食，好喝茶，戒去煙嗜，縱容書癖，每遇好書常傾囊而歸，然於讀書則往往不甚勤苦，且不求甚解，略得輒止。若得三兩至交徜徉于山水之間，必視爲人生之至樂。

于書齋之中，坐擁萬卷書冊，執握一管毛錐，臨池寫畫；暢神盡興之餘，或電話神聊，或擇席小酌，或登山臨水——我能以此爲終老之業，則不虛此生矣。

Autobiography of Xiao Haichun

Xiao Haichun

I was born in March 1944, near the Huangpu River in Shanghai. My ancestors came from Jiangxi province. My late parents were uneducated, and they relied on hard work and thrift They barely made a living on the sea, raising a family of 3 boys and 5 girls, with me being the eldest.

When I was young, I spoke little. My passion was drawing. Over time it became an obsession. Although I was often ticked off by my parents and teachers, I was not swayed from it.

Eventually I attended the Shanghai Arts and Craft School, specializing in jade sculpture. It was to be my only formal training, and my highest education.

The skill might have sounded puny, but I was much blessed by it throughout my life. Studying a piece of jade actually requires wisdom and patience. Merely by creating jade pieces, I have to have the wisdom to adapt, the daring to innovate, the tenacity to labor, and the patience to work ceaselessly. There were days when I was totally adsorbed in my work, such that I forgot about food and sleep. Over time, I became aware of the difference between gain and loss, and be stoical about things.

Later I became involved in painting. There is much fascination in this art. An ancient proverb went like this: "A stone in five days, water in ten." Its essence is in the word "deliberation". "Deliberation" can be explained thus: (1) slowness in anger and frustration; (2) deliberation in studying the work; and (3) understanding does not happen overnight. Understanding the essence enables one not to discredit tradition; nor will it let one's fancy fly. A masterpiece will be crafted at the right moment. That is the difference between a good painting and a bad one. This enlightenment is so personal and profound; it is almost like one has to be a fish in order to know whether the water it is in is warm or cold.

At first I admired Shi Tao and Shi Xi, so I named my studio after them. When I became enchanted with Ba-Da Shan-Ren (1626 -1705), I named it after him ("Snow Embrace Studio"). Yet when I loved Dong Xuanzai, I once again changed its name. Perhaps you will know where my heart is as soon as you have seen the name on my studio.

I am reserved by nature, almost to the point of being stubborn. Although I am not so sociable, I lack few friends. A non-smoker now, my better pleasures are good food, good cup of tea and books. Many times I emptied my wallet on books. Despite that, I am not so particular about thoroughly understanding them. My greatest love is to travel the country with some of my best friends.

I am now totally contented with the little things in life. Whether it be reading my little collection of books in my studio, or painting to my heart's content, or even chatting on the telephone, or perhaps sitting around with my friends, or taking in the breathtaking view of nature, I am satisfied that I have lived a full life.

序

文◎張平沼
金鼎文教基金會 董事長

我十多年前就非常欣賞蕭海春的山水畫，但一直沒有機會與他本人直接晤面暢談繪畫的心得。這些年我常在台灣、大陸兩地往來訪察，每到一個地方，總會抽空到當地的博物館、美術館去走一走，並與有品味的藝術家或收藏家來往。有幸，二年前經好友洪平濤先生的介紹，終於見到了蕭海春先生，彼此之間眞是一見如故，暢談甚歡，從此結下不解之緣。

蕭海春是個很認眞的畫家，他默默耕耘，在書畫上用功數十年。我特別到他的畫室看他作畫，初次見面，他一開始拿出幾張畫給我看，我們一面看一面聊，聊得十分投機。蕭海春畫畫的時候，是先在心中打好稿，動筆後速度便很快，畫面上則慣用層層堆積的手法。尤其是金箔紙，較不容易讓墨色沾上去，墨色要一層層疊畫上去。他畫面上的樹石山林，都需層層渲染、堆疊，由近到遠，有時候要畫上數次，顏色才能夠畫上去，才得以創出主次明暗、濃淡的調子，這樣的畫法是很費力費時的。

從蕭海春的畫中，可看出他在傳統筆墨上建基深厚。這幾年來，他的畫表現出強烈的個人特色。他的構圖多變化，不論是大小幅的作品，都顯出不凡的氣勢。尤其是他的水墨畫，以紮實的筆墨技藝爲根基，以胸有丘壑的情懷爲視界，以對藝術的執著追求爲出發點，推陳出新，另闢蹊徑。另一方面對運用傳統媒材的傳統繪畫創作者而言，中國繪畫擁有幾千年傳統，繪畫技法齊備，名家輩出，因此欲在此基礎上尋求創新，比之西畫更難。以中國傳統繪畫而言，筆與墨是繪畫的精髓，有筆無墨或有墨無筆，都不能算是傳統繪畫。因此筆墨是中國繪畫傳統中，最富價値的內涵之一。而筆墨之妙，正是蕭海春山水畫的特點。

蕭海春的藝術，在當代水墨山水畫的發展上，再一次創造了一番氣勢沉厚的新格局。他憑著孜孜不倦的探索，及敢於創新的膽識和執著，由研究傳統水墨出發，繼而進行寫生創作。同時結合西洋繪畫手法，併用新舊技巧，終能以其深厚的筆墨功夫，創作出中國山水畫的新面貌。尤其是他的大幅作品，誠如評論家李小山先生所說的「層層疊疊的山麓，飛流湧動的雲霧，密密匝匝的樹叢，每一幅作品都如此嚴謹認眞，難以想像，他這麼多作品要花去多少作畫時間。」蕭海春這幾年在香港、新加坡、美國都展出過。在台灣，他也曾在敦煌藝術中心辦過展覽。但是此次能在國家級的歷史博物館展出，對蕭海春而言，是更高層次的肯定，這次展覽雖花了我很多的時間與精力，但想到能邀他到台灣寶島參觀訪問，親自參加畫展的開幕式，也讓台灣的觀眾一同欣賞他的偉大畫作，更是別具意義。

PREFACE

Zhang Pingzhao
Chairman of Jing Ding Foundation

I have admired the landscape paintings of Xiao Haichun for over a decade, but never had the chance of meeting him in person to talk about art. In recent years I have traveled a lot between Taiwan and Mainland China, which gave me the opportunity to visit local museums, art galleries and become acquainted with many discerning artists or collectors. Two years ago, I had the great honor of being introduced to Mr. Xiao through my good friend Hung Pingtao. We connected immediately as if we have known each other for years, and have kept in touch since then.

Xiao is a very serious artist, working quietly over the years at his knowledge and technique of calligraphy and painting. I visited him at his studio and, although it was our first meeting, he showed me several pieces of his work. We looked through them and talked very agreeably. Xiao paints by first making a draft in his head, and realizes the ideas on paper rather quickly, usually through many layers. When working with gold foil paper, it is difficult for the color to sink in and one has to paint layer by layer. In Xiao's work, the trees, rocks and mountains are all presented through many layers of color which are piled on gradually. Sometimes the process has to be repeated many times for the color to stay, so as to create the sense of distance, light and dark tones, primary and secondary shades. This method of painting requires much time and effort.

From Xiao's paintings it is clear that he has a solid command of traditional techniques. Lately the works have displayed strong personal qualities. His extraordinary artistic spirit can be seen in the many varied compositions, regardless of size. The ink paintings, in particular, motivated by Xiao's unwavering pursuit of Art, are created with virtuosic brushworks to represent broad-minded, magnanimous visions; they renew themselves and break new grounds. This is no mean feat, considering the thousands of years of history and highly developed techniques of Chinese painting, as well as the many past masters. As a matter of fact, to be original in such a traditional medium must be even more difficult than in Western art. In traditional Chinese painting, brushstrokes are the bone and sinew, ink work the flesh and blood - a painter wanting in one or the other cannot be regarded as a true artist. Brushstrokes and ink work is the most valuable heritage of the Chinese painting tradition. And the value of Xiao Haichun's landscape paintings lies precisely in the beauty of his brushstrokes and ink work.

Xiao Haichun's artistry has created a fresh perspective for the development of contemporary landscape ink paintings that is noted for its vision and profundity.

Through dedicated explorations and courageous insistent inventions, Xiao crossed into sketching with his understanding of traditional ink painting, combining Chinese and Western painting methods, merging new and old techniques to outline the new face of Chinese landscape painting. His larger works are best described by the critic Li Xiaoshan, "The foot of the mountain range after range; the cloud and mist flying and flowing; the trees and bushes, dense and close... Each piece is painted with such rigor and seriousness that one cannot imagine how much time he took to produce so many works." Over the past few years, Xiao has put on exhibitions in Hong Kong, Singapore and the US; in Taiwan his works have also been shown at Caves Art Center. However, this exhibition at the National Museum of History further consolidates Xiao's status. Although the exhibition has demanded a great deal of time and energy from me, I am extremely pleased to be given the possibility of inviting him to Taiwan for a visit, and to open the exhibition himself. It is also highly significant that art lovers in Taiwan will now be able to appreciate these masterpieces.

說一道一

文◎李小山
中國藝評家

蕭海春以其罕見的深厚功力及傳統素養在當代中國畫壇獨樹一幟。在我的視野裡，當代中國畫壇的傳統守衛者大多是些與傳統毫無關係的人士，他們雖然高喊傳統，擺出一副傳統衛道士的面孔，卻與傳統南轅北轍，因爲他們根本不願意深入到傳統中去，不肯在研究傳統精粹上下工夫，他們照搬幾筆傳統的筆墨，依樣畫葫蘆鋪排出傳統的表面樣式，便敢於以傳統的傳人自居了，中國畫壇所充斥的淺薄、浮躁、喧嘩和炒作，改深深損害了傳統藝術的根基，使之有進一步朽爛的可能。因此，蕭海春在當代中國畫壇的作用自然而然地凸現出來，在一定程度上，由於他的努力，傳統中國畫在我們今天的生活中，仍然顯出它可愛和可敬的一面。

在若干年前，我曾對中國畫痛加撻伐，指出其窮途末路的病源，我的本意是提倡畫家應該與時代溝通，不膜拜在古人和傳統蔭蔽之下，特別指出畫家的創新意識是關鍵所在，我的針對性非常明確，即當時那種濃厚的令人窒息的封閉氣氛，那種保守僵化的現實環境，它們對創新、對開放、對傳統本身都是極其有害的。時至今日，整個藝術領域的多元化，多樣性局面早已形成，各種各樣的藝術樣式都可以大搖大擺地粉墨登場，一方面說明我們面臨的政治文化氛圍的寬鬆，另一方面也說明藝術在當今生活中的必然趨向，定於一尊的權威主義時代過去了，多元化、多樣性的存在成了社會主流。當然，不自由和自由所付出的代價都是與其背景相關聯的，正如在定於一尊的權威主義時代，帶著鐐銬跳舞的藝術也產生過里程碑式輝煌，而在開放的自由的時代，藝術並沒有想像得那麼活力四射，更不要說，在我們的面前，新的金錢至上的權威正在形成強有力的統治，使得大批藝術家成了金錢的奴隸。吳冠中先生說，以前是政治強姦藝術，現在是市場強姦藝術，話雖刺耳，卻是一語中的。但是，我想補充一點，當代畫壇的諸種怪現狀只是社會轉型時期的必然產物，對比之下，無論就創作的自由或空間，還是畫家自身的選擇餘地，都不可與以往同日而語。

如果說在若干年前，一個畫家不研究傳統，不從傳統中截取樣式，會被人指責爲膚淺、浮華或缺乏根基，而在今天，一個畫家依舊堅守傳統，並在傳統_繼續挖掘，會被人指責爲保守、僵化和與時代脫節。說明對畫家的評價取決於語境的不同。只要稍加注意，人們便可發覺，老老少少的畫壇人士，不管他是否樂意和眞誠，“創新”已經成了一個標誌，“新”即“好”這樣的奇談怪論被人奉爲聖典，毫無疑問，從藝術史的演變、發展的軌跡看，創新是關鍵，只有創新才能促使藝術保持活力和新鮮，缺乏創新必將使藝術夭折，而當我們依據這一抽象的觀念看待問題，似乎結論是不言自明的，這讓我想起庫恩對科學革命的理論分析，“革命”與“常態”之間的平衡關係，沒有適當的高平臺的“常態”，“革命”的發生將是一種強扭的瓜，正像許多年來我們所見到的，在“創新”旗幟下出現了多少笑語和鬧劇。

我得趕緊收回這個話題，以免造成誤解，因爲藝術是我們對於存在的夢想之一，是我們探索存在意義的方式之一，按其指向，所有的重複都不會在藝術史上生效，所以，若評判某個畫家的成敗得失，首先是看他爲藝術史貢獻了什麼。然而貢獻並非都是由創新而來，倘若某個畫家能夠成爲他的時代的一個參照系統，也是貢獻的一種，追逐時尚，跟隨大流亦步亦趨，這樣的畫家不可能有作爲，在信古復古時期高喊傳統萬歲，到了今天卻來了個一百八十度轉彎叫嚷起創新，本身就令人懷疑其動機，別說在畫藝上値得期待了，我讚賞蕭海春的品格，從表面看，他是以不變應萬變，爲人處事極爲低調，兩耳不聞窗外事，一心專畫他的畫，而從深層次看，他的不變他的低調，恰恰應合了多元化，多樣性的時代風貌，反而在雜亂無章的局面中凸現出來。這一點，讓我想起中國現代文藝史上的一些有趣事例，當時的眾多大喊“革命”口號的文藝家，一個個煙消雲散，倒是那些默默耕耘的作家和畫家名留青史，有時候，歷史很喜歡拿人們開這樣的開玩笑。

蕭海春奮力在傳統中國畫的領地挖掘，意在表明他幾乎鐵了心要與傳統共存亡。歷年來，對於傳統的爭論夠多了，對於什麼是傳統，如何繼承傳統和發揚傳統的意見眾說紛紜，其實，一切抽象的理論爭論都只提供給我們實踐的背景。我以爲，傳統本身是沒有問題的，正如歷史作爲一個自然的發展過程，它給了我們一把理解現實的鑰匙，關鍵是怎樣打開現實之門，從中找出相互間的聯繫。觀賞蕭海春的作品，猶如觀賞許多古典畫家的作品彙集，從石溪、石濤、漸江、龔賢等往上推，清代、明代、元代乃至宋代的諸大家，均在他作品裡出沒。特別是，蕭海春在多種技巧的運用上，展示出了爐火純青的工夫，這種工夫不是一般畫家照搬幾筆古人的技法所能做到，首先是深刻體驗，在傳統的精粹中吸收養分，從普遍到局部，從局部到普遍，將精神體驗與手上工夫天衣無縫地結合起來，從而將自身的悟性提升到一個很高的位置。我想附帶指出，在眼下的多數中國畫家的筆下，浸染著致命的文人畫習氣，所謂的寫意，所謂的筆墨，所謂神似等等，把畫面該具備的結構、章法、造型和視覺效果掃得一乾二淨。我一看到那種賣弄筆墨，賣弄才情的作品便心生反感，一位專門研究中國畫的美國學者曾對我說，從中國美術史的角度看，是文人畫損害了中國畫的發展，此觀點雖不乏偏激，但也不無道理。

具體分析，蕭海春作品的特點之一是墨色的無窮變化，因爲從章法、佈局和結構上看，他並無脫離傳統山水畫的固定程式，這是否缺憾抑或優點姑且不論，中國山水畫自形成到高度成熟，萬變不離其宗，每一個時期的大師大畫家都沒有偏離過程式，中國畫（山水、花鳥、人物）說到底便是一種較爲純粹的程式化的畫種，像京劇和一些地方戲劇一樣，它的趣味，它的價值和可能性全在程式的限制和範圍之中。所以，當我說到蕭海春作品的墨色時，其實是指它他中國畫程式裡的精彩發揮，同樣，由於蕭海春作品屏棄文人畫習氣，因此顯示出非常嚴謹和細微的描繪，他用大力氣研究墨色，爲的是使得畫面富有縱深感和塑造感，他的畫面給人以一種渾厚、通透、結實和空靈的感受，巧妙地避免了許多畫家在運用重墨時所犯的刻板、僵硬的毛病。蕭海春自覺地選擇了人們常說的“南宗"、山水的渲染方式，山石、樹林、流水、雲霞，都顯得水汽淋漓，從中可以追根尋源，隱約地發現他在學習傳統時的大致脈絡。我們觀賞宋元山水畫，常常會看到，有的畫家故意讓墨色吞吃用筆和線條，逼其服從整體造型的需要，在蕭海春作品裡，我們又一次完整地領略到了這一點。

蕭海春作品的另一特點是章法、結構的張力，記得有一次，我在他畫室裡看到他那些大幅作品，不由受到震動，層層疊疊的山麓，飛流湧動的雲霧，密密匝匝的樹叢，每一幅作品都如此嚴謹認眞，難以想像，他這麼多作品要花多少作畫時間，我見慣了所謂的逸筆草草，見慣了大筆一揮的裝模作樣，面對蕭海春這樣的作品，確是心生敬意。我曾在文章上談過有關保守的問題，對那幫高喊堅守傳統的人予以回擊，即使僅僅從字面上理解，保守也得有東西可保可守，但很多人的保守只保著守著無知二字。蕭海春對章法、結構上的獨特心得，來自於他對畫面整體視覺效果的追求，一方面，說明他對嚮往的自然山景了然於胸，另一方面，說明他眞正吃透了傳統山水畫在章法、結構的精粹。中國山水畫的偉大之處，即是它能將千山萬壑集於一畫之中，將自然形態概括爲視覺程式，所謂“胸中丘壑”正是兩者結合的形態。中國山水畫在歷史過程中逐漸發展爲一個非常完備的系統，獨特的審美趨向和美學意義，與世界上任何畫種拉開了距離。潘天壽曾宣稱，中國繪畫應當與西方繪畫走不同的道路，不僅不能越走越近，相反應該越走越遠，這一觀點作爲一種中西方繪畫比較的詮釋，未被引起足夠重視。一般流行的概念是中西交融，或稱中西合璧，就實踐的事實而言，很難草草下一結論，但是，如前所說，本著傳統中國畫這個獨特系統的所有內在結構早已完備，打破它，改造它或重建它，其結果都可能是削弱它。若干年前，我在一篇文章中呼籲，必須保持中國畫的純潔性，否則將會在創新的口號下取消它，實際上，在多元化、多樣性的時代，某個畫種的純潔性是其價值及意義的保證，我對蕭海春作品抱有敬意，這是原因之一。蕭海春的山水章法、結構不全是出於傳統的技術層面，還有一部份出自他作爲畫家的個性化自覺追求，他喜歡大場面、大境界、大自然、大山水、他的畫面森森然然，自然氣息濃烈，山色水氣逼人，無疑，他所受的傳統技法的啓迪和影響是顯著的，但他在表達上，傳統山水畫的章法、結構只是幫助他構造一座從技到道的橋樑。

這便是蕭海春著重與技法研究的根源所在，技與道之關係，很多人都能說得天花亂墜，但是他們無法付諸於實踐，因爲技的要求並非如常人認爲的那樣簡單，技的磨練需要數十年埋頭苦幹，需要長時間的嘔心瀝血蟄伏，李可染說廢畫三千，不只表明一個數據，一個畫家在實踐中的困頓和付出，不是用多少廢畫來計算。我稱蕭海春在當代中國畫壇爲罕見，至少在勤奮認眞的勁頭上很少有人與他比肩，他的畫作的數量令人難以置信，正說明他所掌握的高度技法眞正可用冰凍三尺非一日之寒來形容。我還認爲，技法到達一定的程度，本身就可以當作觀念來對待，技即是道，道即是技，兩者是密不可分的一個完整的整體，無論在西方繪畫史上或是在中國繪畫史上均能找到許多事例。

現在，蕭海春正屬創作的黃金年齡，有一次我與他開玩笑說，齊白石在你的年齡才開始變法，黃賓虹六十歲時的畫還不算什麼，你卻比他們積累得更紮實。的確，以蕭海春目前的狀況看，我有理由相信，他在未來能夠登頂，儘管他的實踐背景與齊白石、黃賓虹不同，相對而言，齊、黃的活動背景更適宜一些，蕭海春面臨的問題更複雜更難解些，不過，任何成功的畫家都會在自己的存在空間_找到一條正確通道，通向理想之巓。用蕭海春以往的經驗當做一面鏡子，可看到在他筆下，各種各樣的傳統畫法被他品嘗之後結出的果實，繁雜也好，疏簡也好，奇崛也好，平實也好，都顯得那樣的自自然然。我以爲，他的氣處目前爲止還未全部浮現出來，需要時間，時間是偉大的魔術師，時間將使優秀的畫家更加優秀，低劣的畫家遭到無情淘汰。是的，蕭海春正在行進過程中，一些不確定的因素仍會起作用，我的意思是，蕭海春作品的個人面貌和個人圖式仍在形成之中，有的需要加固，有的需要改變，我無法設想他的作品在未來的走向，但我覺得一定是更具強烈個性和衝擊力的，這一點，從他的雄心和耐力便可得知。

(2004.7.6)

A Man of His Word

Li Xiaoshan
Art critic

Xiao Haichun, a man of firm strength of a type that is rarely seen, as well as a man well-cultivated in traditional skills, truly stands alone in contemporary Chinese painting circles. In my view, the majority of defenders of "tradition" in contemporary Chinese painting actually have nothing at all to do with tradition. They may make plenty of racket about their support for "tradition," and parade around in the costumes of "defenders of traditional cultural heritage," but many of their moves are actually in contraction to, or harmful to, their cause. This is simply because they are completely unwilling to truly immerse themselves in real tradition, and unwilling to put forth the energy required to truly research the essentials of the tradition that they claim to be defending. They simply imitate some traditional methods, producing copies with a traditional face yet lacking a traditional essence, and then go so far as to call themselves the descendants of the artistic masters of old. The shallowness, rashness, hubbub, and imitation that permeates Chinese painting circles has caused irreparable harm to the foundations of traditional art, and brought it one step closer to decay. Considering this state of affairs, Xiao Haichun's role in the world of contemporary Chinese painting naturally stands out: to a certain degree, it is on account of his endeavors that traditional Chinese painting is still able to show what remains of its likable and admirable side in our world today.

A couple of years ago, I was harshly critical of Chinese painting. My intention in pointing out the roots of the dead-end faced at the time was to advocate the idea that painters needed to communicate with their era, rather than just sitting and worshipping ancient masters in the shade of tradition. I wanted to emphasize the fact that a creative consciousness is key for painters. The intended target of my discourse was absolutely clear: the stiflingly suffocative closed atmosphere and rigidly conservative environment of the time that was causing great harm to creativity, openness, and even to tradition itself. And today, multi-dimensionality and diversity in the field of art has already been a well-established fact for quite some time now. All different types of art forms and styles have their chance to swagger onto stage in full regalia, coming and going. This, on the one hand, goes to show the openness of our current political and cultural atmosphere, while on the other hand also shows the natural direction that art must follow in our contemporary lives. The authoritarian era of one-man rule is far behind us, and a multi-dimensional and diverse existence has become the mainstream. Of course, there are prices to be paid in both free and closed environments, prices that are determined by the background of the times. Back in the era of authoritarianism, "dancing around in handcuffs" could be remembered as a shining artistic milestone, while in our current freer era, art is not quite as full of life as many would have thought. And I am sure that you all know, without my even mentioning it, that a new form of authoritarian rule is taking shape right before our eyes: rule by money, which is turning a number of artists into slaves to cash. Mr. Wu Guanzhong once said that in the past it was politics that raped art, but that now it is the market that is raping art. While this saying might be a little hard on the ears, there is no denying that it is right in principle. However, I must add that the various bizarre developments that we see nowadays are in fact just natural, unavoidable by-products of this period of social transition. Really, in terms of both creative freedom and artists' room for choices, I think we can all agree that there is simply no way that the past could be compared with the present.

A number of years ago, a painter who did not research tradition or grab a few styles from the traditional palette would be criticized as shallow, showy, and rootless. Nowadays, if a painter holds fast to tradition, and continues to tap the source of tradition, they are criticized as conservative, rigid, or out of step with the times. This just goes to show that assessments are determined by their historical context. All you have to do is look around, and you will realize that all of the figures in today's painting circles, both young and old, have all seen "innovation" become a status symbol, no matter whether they actually agree with this trend or not. This absurd idea that "new" automatically equals "good" has already become a guiding principle for a number of people. Looking back at the history of art, innovation is, without a doubt, key to the process of art's evolution and development. Only with creativity can art maintain its vitality and freshness; a lack of innovation is certain to drive art to an early death. And in looking at issues using this abstract theoretical concept, our conclusions are obvious without having to even say them aloud. This leads me to think of W. Kuhne's theoretical analysis of the scientific revolution, and his commentary on the equilibrium that needs to exist between "the revolution" and "normalcy." Without a suitable platform of "normalcy," any "revolution" is forced. This resembles exactly what we have seen over the last number of years, with countless pure jokes and farces being performed under the flag of "innovation."

I need to take this discourse back, in order to avoid any misunderstandings because art is one of our life dreams, and one of the methods by which we seek out the meaning of life. According to the tenets of the blind praise of innovation, all repetition would be forgotten from the history of art. In evaluating a painter's accomplishments and failures, the first thing you want to look at is the contribution that they made to the history of art. Yet contributions do not all come from "innovation." Should a painter be able to become a model for artistic study in his or her era, this could also be considered a type of contribution. Painters who simply follow trends in fashion and go along with the mainstream could never really accomplish anything. Shouting out "long live tradition" in an era that believed in and repeated traditional styles, and nowadays, continuously going on and on about "innovation" in a 180 degree reversal: this is the type of thing that leaves people with doubts about some artists' intentions; and there is certainly no need to discuss the possibility of wanting to follow such artists' next steps. I deeply admire Xiao Haichun's moral character: on the surface, he is a man who has held steady in the sea of changes around him; he has an especially low-key way of dealing with people and issues; he happens to fit just perfectly with the current multi-dimensional and diverse era, and in fact stands out as a unique figure in the current chaotic environment. This makes me think of an interesting aspect of China's modern literary and artistic history: all of those artists and writers yelling and screaming about "revolution" have disappeared, one after another, from the face of art circles; while it has been those writers and painters that have been diligently working alone on their art that have ever so quietly left their mark on history. History, in fact, loves to play such jokes on us.

Xiao Haichun has put all of his effort into tapping into traditional Chinese painting, showing his determination to live and die with tradition. In recent years, there have been a number of debates about tradition, with various diverse opinions about what tradition is, how to carry on tradition, and how to develop and promote tradition. But all of these abstract theoretical arguments can only serve as a background for our real life experiences. Personally, I feel there is nothing wrong with tradition in itself. Just as history serves as a natural process of development, providing us with the keys to understanding our present reality, tradition does the same. The question is, how do you go about opening this door, and how do you view the relationship between history and our present reality? Appreciating the works of Xiao Haichun is a lot like admiring the collections of classic painters, from Shi Xi, Shi Tao, Jian Jiang, and Gong Xian, on to the many famous painters of the Qing, Ming, Yuan, and even the Song: they all appear in his works. This is especially true with regards to Xiao Haichun's application of a variety of painting techniques, demonstrating his exquisite skills, the type of skills absent in any ordinary painter imitating the works of the masters. First one must gather rich experience, soaking up the nourishment of tradition's essence, going from general traditional methods all the way down to their specific characteristics, and then back to the general, finding a perfect and natural unity between your spiritual experience and your own skills, thus elevating your own power of insight. I would like to add that of the works of the majority of Chinese painters that I have seen, most are permeated with the dangerous habits of "literati painting," with their so-called "impressionistic portrayal," "stylistic strokes," and "spiritual expression." All of this tends to completely wipe out any of the structure, composition, shape, or visual effects that should be incorporated into a painting. It actually makes me sick to view such paintings, showing off with their strokes and their so-called artistic talents. An academic from the United States who researches Chinese art once told me that from the perspective of China's art history, it is just such "men of letters" who have hampered the development of Chinese painting. While this opinion may be a little prejudiced or perhaps even extreme, we must admit that it is not completely lacking in reason.

In a more concrete analysis, one of the traits of Xiao Haichun's paintings that really stands out is their boundless color. Looking at these paintings based on their presentation, layout, and structure, they certainly have not left behind traditional landscape patterns. For the time being, let's not discuss whether this is a strong or weak point. Chinese landscape painting, from its inception all the way through its development into a mature art form, has never left its guiding principles through this sea of changes. The main painters of each and every era have never strayed too far from these traditional patterns. Chinese painting (landscape, bird and flower, character) is a rather purely stylized type of painting, much like Peking Opera or some local theater styles. Its point of interest, its value, and its possibilities, are all within formulated limits. So, when I talk about the colors in Xiao Haichun's paintings, I am actually talking about his brilliant progress strictly within the formula of Chinese painting. As Xiao Haichun's works have cast away the practices of so-called literati paintings, they demonstrate an especially rigorous and subtle artistic portrayal. He has put a lot of effort into researching colors, in hopes of giving his paintings an abundance of depth and shape. His paintings emanate with a feeling of simple and honest sincerity, transparency, solidity, and artistry, ingeniously avoiding the mechanical, rigid feeling of many ink painters. Xiao Haichun consciously chose to follow the well-known Southern School method of applying colors in landscape paintings: his rocks, trees, flowing water, and rosy clouds all feel like they are dripping with dew. From these characteristics, we can trace his art to its roots and understand his course of development in the study of traditional painting. One can often see that some landscape painters of the Song and Yuan Dynasty intentionally made their colors swallow up their strokes and figures, forcing them to obey the overall needs of the entire painting. Xiao Haichun's works give us yet another opportunity to appreciate such methods.

Another unique trait of Xiao Haichun's works is the tension within his presentation and structure. I remember looking at some of his larger works in his studio once, and could not help but feel shocked: layer upon layer of piedmont, the rosy clouds drifting by, the thick treetops.... it is really difficult to imagine just how much time he spent to complete so many detailed and thorough works of art. I have always taken offense at the affected airs of wide, unrestrained strokes, but my heart is filled with respect for the type of art that I see in Xiao Haichun's works. I have already discussed the question of conservatism, and I have this response for those who are carrying on about defending tradition. Simply the word "conservatism" itself implies that there must in fact be something to conserve, something to defend. Yet in fact, most conservatives in the world of painting have only one thing to protect, and that is their sheer ignorance. Xiao Haichun's unique knowledge of both composition and structure comes from his aspiration for completely integrated visual effects in his painting. On the one hand, this goes to show that he has a deep understanding of natural landscape scenes, while on the other hand showing that he has a thorough grasp of the essence of composition and layout in traditional Chinese landscape paintings. The truly amazing thing about Chinese landscape painting is that it is able to squeeze unending mountains and valleys into a single painting, summarizing the infinite shapes of nature in a visual formula. Its strength comes from the unity of nature and its methods. Chinese landscape painting, in the process of historical development, has gradually developed into a complete system, with a unique direction and aesthetic meaning, far removed from any other type of painting in the world. Pan Tian-shou once stated that "Chinese painting should naturally follow a different path than that of Western painting. Not only will they not grow increasingly similar; they should in fact grow farther and farther apart." His point of view has not attracted enough serious consideration as an analysis of the relationship between Chinese and Western painting. Generally, the popular ideas nowadays are "the blending of East and West," or "combining East and West." It is very difficult to casually come up with a final conclusion about this trend simply based on our own experience. But as I said before, the internal structures of the unique system of traditional Chinese painting were complete long ago; breaking or changing these structures can only result in one thing: the weakening of the entire system. In an essay written a number of years ago, I made an appeal for us to maintain the purity of Chinese painting; otherwise, I warned, we will have destroyed it under the banner of "innovation." Really, in a multi-dimensional era of diverse styles, the purity of any type of painting is actually a guarantee of its value and its meaning. This is one of the reasons that I have such deep respect for the works of Xiao Haichun. His landscape presentation and structure are not completely based on traditional skills: some of it comes from his own conscious expressions of individuality. He likes grand, sweeping scenes, Mother Nature, and massive landscapes. His paintings are dense, with a strong flavor of nature, to the point that one can even taste the dew on the mountain in his paintings. The influence and enlightenment that he has received from traditional painting techniques is clearly obvious, yet in his delivery, traditional landscape paintings' presentation and structure simply serve to assist him in constructing a bridge between "technique" and "principles."

This is the reason for Xiao Haichun's emphasis upon researching techniques: the relationship between "techniques" and "principles." There are plenty of people that can talk your ear off about their skills, but are actually unable to survive in the real world of painting, because the demands of mastering techniques are just not as simple as everyone often thinks. Tempering oneself in these techniques requires decades of meticulous practice, an extremely long period of intensive, solitary diligence. Li Keran said that he had produced thousands of paintings that were nothing but trash. This is not just a statistic: rather, it illustrates the price that a painter needs to pay in order to develop his or her skills. But of course this is not a price that can simply be measured in terms of the quantity of paintings produced. I have stated that a painter like Xiao Haichun is a rarity in contemporary Chinese painting circles; there are very few nowadays that could compete with him in terms of diligent strength and dedication. It is hard to believe the number of paintings he has produced; "Rome was not built in a day," he has undergone the extensive training necessary to attain such a strong grasp of painting techniques. In my own opinion, when someone's grasp of techniques reaches a certain level, these techniques develop into the painter's own unique idea: one's "techniques" become "principle," while one's "principles" become a "technique." The two become a single, complete, inseparable body. Plentiful examples of this can found in the history of both Western painting and Eastern painting.

Xiao Haichun is currently in the midst of his creative "golden years." Once I joked with him saying "Qi Baishi was your age before he started to have any influence on the painting world, and Huang Binhong was still producing mediocre paintings at the age of 60. You have actually established a much more solid foundation than either of them." Looking at Xiao Haichun's current situation, I certainly have reason to believe that he will reach the summit of painting. His background experience may be different from that of Qi Baishi and Huang Binhong, and Qi and Huang's background may even be slightly more fitting for the role. Furthermore, the problems Xiao Haichun faces may be more complex and difficult to resolve. But every successful painter must find their correct path in the environment in which they live, the path that will lead them to the peak of their ideals. The results of Xiao Haichun's plentiful experience are clear: the complex, the straightforward, the peculiar, the simple and unadorned, all of these styles seem so natural to him. And in my opinion, his strengths have yet to be fully revealed. This takes time... time is the great magician: outstanding painters become even more outstanding, and inferior painters are mercilessly sifted out from the crowd. Yes, Xiao Haichun is still a work in progress; there are some still unknown factors that could influence his future path of development. The individual character and individual style of Xiao Haichun's works are still taking shape: some of his stylistic traits shall be further consolidated, while some shall change. I am unable to imagine what direction his works will take in the future, but I can say for certain that his works will continue to show a strong sense of individuality and will have a major impact on the painting world; this much I can guarantee from his great ambition and his endurance.

說澄明之境：渾厚華滋——蕭海春特展簡評

文◎邵　琦

山水畫是什麼？

——這是一個問題。

這個問題很久沒有問了，

這個問題很少有人去問。

在文言語境中這個問題不是一個問題，

在白話語境中這個問題始終是一個問題。

當我們面對蕭海春的近作時，上述這些夾雜著“問題”的問題句子便前來照面了，是這樣的具體、真切、直截了當、不可迴避，因此，在評說蕭海春的近作之前，首先要回答這個似是而非的、面熟而陌生的問題。

對於繪畫理論，蕭海春是述而不作的。雖然，他在畫面上時有題跋，且不少還是長題，但所題多是具體而微的體會或感受，顯然不能作爲嚴謹、系統的理論闡述來看待。繪畫的問題用繪畫來思考，這是蕭海春一直的堅持。

於是，他引領我們來到展廳，來到他的作品面前，“作品”和“展廳”之間構成的“呈現”關係本身凸現了這個問題——“山水畫是什麼？”

而我們必須總體地或者整體地接受他的作品的提問，因爲作品就是問題中的“什麼”。在這個展廳中，不是具體某一件作品在提問，而是這些作品給我們提供的直接的視覺經驗和由這些視覺經驗引發的我們固有的關於山水畫的歷史和現狀的認知與觀念激活了問題。這_所謂的“歷史”是指最遲從謝赫、王微、展子虔以來的以山川林木爲題材的繪畫作品和理論；所謂的“現狀”則是指從康有爲、陳獨秀大革“王畫”的命以來的以山川林木爲題材的繪畫作品和理論。前者我們可以說是繪畫的“文言語境”，後者我們可以說是繪畫的“白話語境”。在“文言語境”中，“山水畫是什麼？”並沒有以問題的方式出現或存在，在“白話語境”中，“山水畫是什麼？”則是被誤讀或被懸擱的問題。

在由蕭海春的作品構成的特定範圍——展覽中，這個被激活了的問題如此直接地前來照面，源于蕭海春的作品共時性地展示了“白話語境”和“文言語境”——在這個消弭了時間隔斷的空間_，古老的問題在一個新的基礎上以歷史連續性的身份在當下獲得了尋求解答的權利。這個新的基礎不僅是指對“白話語境”和“文言語境”的整合，同時也包括了對以西方爲代表的“注音語境”一個多世紀以來的對“白話語境”的建構所產生的影響和作用（包括正面和負面）的認知和理解。

蕭海春建構這一新基礎的方法是對經典作品的臨寫。

臨寫對蕭海春來說是一種“手談”。當一個人面對一些根本問題並企圖尋究解答時，最需要是對手之間的交流和溝通。伯牙在鍾子期死後不再鼓琴是無奈，尼爾斯_玻爾在愛因斯坦死後依然把他當作科學研究上的對手同樣是無奈。在普遍地懸擱“山水畫是什麼”的“白話語境”中，蕭海春更願意和歷史上大家巨擘們商討——仿彿棋手在尋求對手、尋求和對手的交流；不需要語言的“手談”，在繪畫動作的重演中體會、揣摩、感悟、交流。

在這種動作重演中體會情懷、揣摩心思，感悟造化，進而交流心得、獲得激情。因此，從董源、巨然、范寬、李成、郭熙、趙孟頫、黃公望、黃鎮、倪瓚、王蒙、文徵明、沈周、董其昌到王時敏、王鑒、王翬、王原祁、石濤、八大山人、髡殘、龔賢~~用手更用心重演，並從重演中贏獲山水畫的歷史連續性。因此，蕭海春的臨寫作品中或惟妙惟肖，或得意忘形，一一昭示的都是畫家在不同心境和情境的所悟所得。

蕭海春的臨寫不僅洗去了堆積在這些經典作品上的斑駁漬痕和塵埃，而且消除了阻隔這些歷史大家進入當下的門牆——我們似乎聽到了一個齊齊的聲音：二十一世紀的人們，你們說山水畫是什麼？

臨寫的結果是畫面、是形象、是筆墨，在這裡，畫面、形象、筆墨也是蕭海春和歷史交流的眞實記載。

面對蕭海春的這一系列臨寫作品，我們也就獲得了審視"文言語境"中對"山水畫是什麼"的解答的別一角度。"暢神"是"文言語境"中對"山水畫是什麼"解答，並且是根本性的解答。這一解答的玄奧之處於：在山水畫幼稚的草創時期，我們就擁有了如此簡明而圓滿的解答。沒有過程，也不需要積累，似乎是淩空而來。並且，宗炳用了"暢神而已"這樣一種不容置疑的肯定句式，強調了其唯一性。此外，緊接而來的一聲歎問："神之所暢，孰有先焉？"幾乎爲所有的後來者免去了詰問——"山水畫是什麼"這一不可迴避的根本問題的煩勞。換言之，"暢神"作爲"山水畫是什麼"這一問題的根本層面上的解答，雖然是宗炳給出的，但是，在以後的歷史進程中，成爲人們的共識，卻不能說是宗炳個人強加給後來的結果，恰恰相反，它是後人共同選擇的必然。長久以來人們不問這個問題，不是這個問題不存在，而是這個問題的解答始終穿越時空成爲每個不同時期的每一個個人現成的解答。"暢神"既可在創作過程中體悟，也可在欣賞過程中體悟，只是這"體悟"每個具體的個人來說都必須親身參與中贏得，並且是他人無法替代的獨自贏得。宗炳所謂"神之所暢，孰有先焉。"其本義正在此。因而，"暢神"在"六法"的技術支撐下獲得了規導百代的成效。

"暢神"不是邏輯陳述，而是動作體悟，這體悟或深或淺、或高或低，因人而異，而人們不同的體悟又在不同的時間點上共同豐富著（個性鮮明的）落實著（個性平實的）山水畫的根本解答。

建立在動作基礎上的技法的精深與完備過程，使山水畫漸次獲得了納入到"技可進乎道"的民族思維性格之中的資格。倪瓚的"胸中逸氣"經過後人有意味的誤讀後，可以看成是一個標誌；而嗣後董其昌"畫之道，所謂宇宙在乎手者，眼前無非生機。"則是一次承前啓後的總結。

"生機"是暢神的具體，也是"氣韻"的具體。"生機"是繪畫的狀態，也是畫家的狀態。從這個時候起，中國山水畫進入了無可無不可的自由境界。從這個時候起，時間中累積起來的一切都共同地成爲歷史支援，進退取捨，一任由己。

這是山水畫呈示其歷史連續性的本因。歷史連續性所指的便是：具有空間性質的根本上的趨同一致和具有時間性質的筆墨上的各具面目，換言之，以“暢神”爲指歸的筆墨形色不僅構成了山水畫，而且，構成了山水畫的歷史。因而，山水畫的歷史不僅在時間性狀上的是連續的，同時，在空間形態上是包容的。

當蕭海春以“臨寫”的方式投入歷史時，歷史便在它的面前呈現爲一方富饒的綠洲。

在這一歷史的富饒領域中，蕭海春循依著個我心性，攫取了渾厚華滋。

在蕭海春看來，“渾厚華滋”是山水畫正脈的具體體現，也是自然生機之所在。探究自然生機是蕭海春山水的孜孜以求。在渾樸、敦厚、華茂、滋醇的畫面背後，交響著是依偎于自然的亙古心曲。

蕭海春的山水畫是單純的，除了泉石、林木、煙雲，還是泉石、林木、煙雲。然而，這種單純到近乎單一的形象，在蕭海春的層層密密的經營中，猶如賦格曲一樣，引導著人們滌除塵慮，收視反照，突入澄明。

山水畫：面向自然的存在。——肝膽相照，心性相印，表裡俱澄澈。

此時在場的是物質性的畫、也是既定時空點上的人、更是超越時空的山水。當畫以這樣的方式在場時，人是林泉之心，山水是胸中丘壑。畫在這樣的場合落實爲“天人合一”的“一”。這“一”是如此具體，這“一”又是如此虛玄；然而，正是在這具體的虛玄的兩極張力中，無論是老子的“道生一、一生二，二生三，三生萬物”；還是赫拉克_特的“萬物源於一，一源於萬物”，這些平素費解的觀念在這_被理解。

這是傳統。山水的傳統，山水詩的傳統，山水畫的傳統。當孔子在川上感歎的時候，我們看到了這個傳統；當但丁和彼德拉克在登山臨水的時候，我們看到了這個傳統。

蕭海春固然沒有用這樣的文字來做這樣的闡述，但，在蕭海春的畫面上我們卻分明看到了他不僅是這樣理解傳統，而且是這樣擁有傳統。

當畫家經由技法程式悟入藝術根本之後，一如《桃花源記》所說：豁然開朗，進入了一個超然的自由境界。進退取捨，一任由己，而唯一能夠制約的是他的個我心性。

經典的或者說古典的程式或樣式，乃是先賢們在傳統的支援中個我心性的髮露。蕭海春在對經典的臨寫中悟入傳統，在和先賢們的手談中擁有傳統，進而在傳統中的支援中髮露個我心性。

於是，在蕭海春的創作中，我們看到了源遠流長的傳是如何支援著蕭海春，令他在文言語境橫遭隔斷、注音語境強勢侵淩、白話語境曖昧含糊的當下，一以貫之地涵泳山川林木，抒寫胸中丘壑，營構一派渾厚華滋的澄明之境。

筆墨是傳統的承載媒介，因而，傳統的支援也最顯然地體現在筆墨之中。在癸未年（1995）的一部山水冊頁的跋記中，蕭海春有過這樣一段文字，反思自己的創作歷程：“餘昔作畫，多粗率，名之曰：逸筆草草，暢情達意。實落揚州畫派舊徑，筆墨橫塗豎抹，失卻法度。雖有恣肆不羈之氣度，然滿紙疥癩，習氣橫生。觀古人作畫，筆精墨妙，氣息古厚醇靜，非五日一石，十日一水，慘淡經營，不妄下一筆而能，故反思再三，餘要脫盡蹊徑，力避時風，必入古法。在經意處，入古法門徑，浸淫其間。與古法交流有餘年，始知筆墨爲何物。回觀昔作與時下率意多入邪道，非中國畫之正脈。爲計尋覓，另僻新體，故一反常態，出以密體，有別疏體；不出新奇好景，旨在於正脈：以筆墨之妙，妙造自然。”“不出新奇好景”在蕭海春實際上是排卻了山水畫在山水之外，所謂“意義”、“價値”、“功用”等等之類非山水根本意蘊的干擾，歸入於山水本然——“始知筆墨爲何物”，進而，展開其以筆墨之妙，妙造自然的“新體”創作。

具體而論，蕭海春的用筆由任性的恣肆向循性的醇厚斂歸。亦即在獲取石濤、八大山人酣暢淋漓的同時，上追原由，從清初的“四王”（王時敏、王鑒、王翬、王原祁）到明末的董其昌；從元季四大家（黃公望、吳鎮、倪瓚、王蒙）到元初的趙孟頫、高克恭；從宋代的范寬、郭熙到五代的董源、巨然，循流探源，心摹手追。在保持披麻皴以流暢的中鋒長線爲本色的基礎上，循依渾樸之旨，陶鑄成自己腴潤醇厚的筆線特徵。

至於用墨，蕭海春早年便行黃賓虹的墨法中悟得三昧，因此有“黑色調”山水時期。雖然這一時期的作品有深雄壯闊之氣，卻于華滋流韻猶有所憾。源于黃賓虹墨法的啓迪，更源于黃賓虹畫史的學識，蕭海春返求歷史，由龔賢到吳鎮，由高克恭到“二米”，上下求證，在“運墨而五色俱”的法則下，領悟水墨的“黑色”在中國文化中所獨有的幽昧、緬邈、深遠的意蘊。

筆墨本不可分，筆即墨，墨即筆，勾、皴、點、染，都必須筆墨互見，共同奠定畫面的根基：亦即賦予畫面的形象以個我的心性特質。這正是山水畫暢心達性的“暢神”旨歸之所。如果斤斤於形象的輪廓外形的還原眞實，難免爲物所拘囿——“文言語境”所謂：“畫界魔師”“工匠”是也，山水畫所描繪的固然是山川林木，更是胸中丘壑，而這經由心靈陶冶而就的胸中丘壑如何落實爲紙素上的山川林木，用理論的語句說是以筆墨之妙，妙造自然，從技法的角度說是以具有心性特質的形象構成元素聚積並由此凸現形象的心性特質，而輪廓外形的差異當退爲其次。蕭海春所說的“新體”之“新”意正在於此；而“始知筆墨爲何物”之“物”也在這_得到呈現。

基於此，我們也就獲得了考究畫面形象的可能。

畫面形象對畫家來說是創作的最後結果，對觀者來說是觀賞的最初印象。蕭海春的畫面形象向以雄渾的氣格名世。大山大水，大丘大壑，長松巨木，煙雲變幻，鋪天塞地，密密匝匝、層層疊疊，眞力彌漫而生機鬱勃。在盈丈巨幅中，我們可以感受撲面而來的壓迫感；在巴掌大的小品中，我們同樣可以感受彌漫的巨大張力。換言之，蕭海春以他的繪畫創作表明：畫面氣象和畫面的大小是沒有邏輯關聯的；畫面的氣象乃是由畫家的胸次所決定的。而又從另一個角度印證：山水畫不僅是山川林木的表現，更全是胸中丘壑的表達。

在形象刻畫或經營位置上，在蕭海春看來：平遠、高遠、深遠的“三遠”法則更適合胸中丘壑的自由不拘的表達。“三遠”有點籠統、有點含糊，當然不夠科學，但是，這一點籠統和含糊，卻正好精確地應對了胸中丘壑的特點。正如生活中最精確的、最人性化的、也是最“科學”的數學是“模糊數學”一樣。惟其如此，蕭海春才擁有這樣一份自由和自在：循依內心的引導妙造自然。

當然，渾厚華滋不是一個“大”字可以涵蓋的，蕭海春的雄渾氣象實際上是由腴潤醇厚的筆墨雕塑而就的。由於蕭海春早年曾從事玉雕，並獲得國家藝術大師的稱號，因此，對於他畫面中程現的雕塑體量感，人們多願意行他早年的藝術經歷中去尋求原因。無疑，人生的經歷尤其是藝術經歷，總會以某種方式在其日後的藝術創作中流露，但是，蕭海春畫面上的體量感卻不是由三維的雕塑經驗遷移過來的，而是由筆墨自身的圓渾質感建構起來的。非常直接的視覺經驗告訴我們：蕭海春的畫面形象並不追求所謂的透視效果，這一點甚至他是放棄或排斥的。因爲，在層層疊疊的山石堆疊中，形象的結構邏輯是近乎二維平面性的。倘若能用現代構成的眼光來看，這一特點或許可以得到比較貼切的解析。此外，我們也可以從文言語境中的王原祁的畫面中，或者從稍稍類似可以進行平行比照的注音語境_的塞尙的畫面中看到普遍存在於繪畫中的這種形象描繪特質。

如果確實要尋找出蕭海春早年從事玉雕的藝術經歷對他現在繪畫創作的影響或作用，倒是覺得他在色彩的感覺上始終對美玉的溫潤幽媚難以釋懷，也正是這一點，使蕭海春的畫面在雅渾的陽剛之中始終透溢出一份秀逸的陰柔。玉的性質堅而脆，玉的感覺溫而潤，至剛至柔的合爲一體——從玉的這一特性中，蕭海春具體地領悟到藝術的辯證法，同時行山水畫的歷史中得到印證：所謂雲林（倪瓚）之“簡”，其要旨在“密”；山樵（王蒙）之“繁”，其要旨在疏；煙客（王時敏）之“老”，其要旨在“秀”；耕煙（王原祁）之“嫩”，其要旨在“蒼”。因此，蕭海春畫面上的那一份陰柔之美，僅僅從技法層面上來揭示是不夠的，同時也是膚表的。正是有了這樣剛柔並濟的遒韌品格，大山大水，才能融入胸中、發爲丘壑我們可以這樣說，如果沒有色彩上的溫潤幽媚，蕭海春的雄渾深沈不會有如此的汪洋恣肆的藝術張力和郁勃盛茂的生機活力。

“胸中丘壑”是“自然山水”的澄明之象，因而，這種得之於心源的形象，始終都是由然不拘的，自然流暢的。如果我們願意拋棄那些以時間爲隔板分割新舊，並將新舊套入進化論來決定生機活力的非歷史性的解構手段，居於傳統之中並在傳統的支援之中，拆除門牆，消弭時滯，照面作品，那麼，品評就會出席，標準就會在場，不再失措彷徨的我們就可以在晉唐之間取捨，在宋元之間漫步，在明清之間進退，在中西之間兼趣⋯當歷史成爲沒有任何附加前提或條件的備擇資源時，我們便擁有了自由——只屬於當今的自由。中西古今、晉唐宋元等等一概都是抽去了用圖像標定的時間之後的並列共存——這便是傳統的襟懷、山水的精神。

“山水畫是什麼？”——如果說山水畫或者說中國繪畫眞的像人們所認定的那樣：一個世紀以來抑或是幾個世紀以來一直就處於困境之中，那麼，這種莫名的困境將會在這樣的詰問中獲得轉機。

“山水畫是什麼？”——如果說這是蕭海春一直堅持用繪畫來思考著的一個繪畫的問題，那麼，他的思考本身：那一方渾厚華滋的山水天地，就已經以“是”的方式證明了“什麼”。

A State of Clearness: Magnificent and Smooth

—— A Brief Commentary on the Special Exhibition of Xiao Haichun's Work of Art

Shao Qi

What is the "landscape painting"?
This is a question...

...A question that has not been asked for a long time.
...A question that hardly anyone asks these days.

In the context of the old Chinese language, this question is not a question.
In the context of the modern Chinese language, this question remains a question.

When we look at the recent work by Xian Haichun, we are approached by the above problematic "question". This question is so concrete, true and direct that we cannot avoid. Therefore, before we being to comment on Xiao's recent work, we first have to answer this familiar and yet strange question.

Xiao describes the theory of painting instead of "building" it. Although he writes short passages on his paintings (and many of them are long ones), he mostly writes about his experience or feelings. Therefore, these short passages cannot be treated as a serious and systematic theory. Moreover, Xiao has always insisted that the questions of painting be contemplated with paintings.

With this mindset, he leads us into the exhibition halls, to stand before his work of art. The "representation" of the "work" and the "exhibition hall" highlights the question - "What is the landscape painting"?

Overall, we have to totally accept the questions from his work, as the work is the "what" in the question. In this exhibition hall, no single piece of work is asking any question. Instead, all of the masterpieces are providing us direct visual experiences. These experiences inspire us to have knowledge and concepts about the history and current situation of the landscape paintings, and thus bring up the question. The so-called "history" mentioned here refers to the paintings and theories with the subjects of mountains, rivers and forests since the age of Xie He, Wang Wei and Zhan Zi Qian, while the "current situation" refers to those since Kang Youwei and Chen Duxiou revolutionized the art of painting. We can call the former one "the context of the old Chinese language" of painting, while the latter can be dubbed as the context of the modern Chinese language. "What is the landscape painting" in the "old Chinese language context"? This "question" does not emerge or exist in any way of "a question". "What is the landscape painting" in the "modern Chinese language context"? This is a question that is often mis-interpreted or ignored.

In the special range - the exhibition - that is formed by Xiao's work, this question approaches us so directly6. Moreover, Xiao's work concurrently displays both contexts. In the space in which the division of the time period is removed, this old question, based on a new foundation, is given the right to search for an answer as a subject of the continuity of history. The new foundation not only refers to the integration of the two contexts, it also includes the concepts and understanding of the influences and impacts (both positive and negative) that the "phonetic" context, represented by the Western world, has had on the construction of the modern Chinese language context.

The way that Xiao Haichun uses to build this new foundation is to "imitate" the classic masterpieces.

Imitation, for Xiao, is a way to "talk by hands". When we face some fundamental questions are try to look for an answer, what we need the most is the exchanges and communications with our counterparts. After the death of Zhong Ziqi, Be Ya stopped playing the music. After Albert Einstein died, Niels Bohr still saw him as a respectful rival in terms of scientific researches. In the context of the modern Chinese language that usually tends to ignore the question "what is the landscape painting?", Xiao Haichun is more willing to discuss with masters throughout history, as if he is searching for counterparts and exchanges and communications with them. This is the kind of "talking by hands" that needs no language but to experience, feel, imitate and communicate when repeating the movements of painting a piece of work.

Through this, artists experience, imitate and feel the senses and concepts of the painting, and then exchange what they have learned and thus obtained their passion. Therefore, all painters in the history "imitate" with hands and more with heart. And they regain the continuity of the history by imitating. Thus, Xiao's work of imitation is so vivid or wild, showing the thoughts and experiences that painters have in different contexts and moods.

Xiao's imitation have not only washed away the stains and dust that piled on these classics, it also has eliminated the barriers that kept these masters from entering the modern time. We seem to have heard a voice that is asking us: people of the 21st century, what do you think a landscape painting is?

The results of the imitation are the paintings, images and the ink. In here, the so-called "painting, image and ink" is the true account of Xiao's communication with the history.

By looking at Xiao's imitation work, we get a new perspective of the answer to "what is the landscape painting" in the "old Chinese language context". "Spirit-lifting" is the answer, and it is a fundamental one. The wonder about this answer is: in the childhood of the landscape paintings, we already had such a simple and satisfying answer. It needed no process or accumulation of experiences. It just appeared. Moreover, Zong Bing used a positive phrase -- "nothing but spirit-lifting" - to emphasize on its exclusiveness. This is followed by a sigh and yet another question: "When considering the smooth, unimpeded action of the gods, how can there be any question of precedence?" This question saved all followers the trouble to ask the unavoidable question: "what is the landscape painting?" In other words, Zong Bing provided the answer. This answer has become the consensus among people during the progression of history. We cannot see it as the result of Zong Bing's effort. On the contrary, it is the certainty that the followers chose together. The reason that this question has not been asked for a long time is not that this question does not exist. It is because the answer to this question has transcended the boundary of time and become a common answer for people in different periods of time. "Spirit-lifting" can both be experienced in the processes of creation and appreciation. However, we have to take part in it personally to "experience" it. Other people cannot earn the experience for us. And this is exactly the meaning of the phrase "When considering the smooth, unimpeded action of the gods, how can there be any question of precedence?". As a result, with the support of the "six methods", "spirit-lifting" gained the effects to regulate artists throughout the entire history.

"Spirit-lifting" is not a logical description but an understanding of the movements. Such kind of the understanding can be deep or shallow, high or low, depending on different personalities of people. In addition, understandings from different people having been enriching the fundamental answer in a vivid or plain way.

The profound and comprehensive process of techniques that are built upon the basis of movements has given the landscape painting the entry ticket to be incorporated in the Chinese idea of "improve the technique and make it "Dao" (way)". Ni Zan's painting was purposefully mis-interpreted by people of a later period of time, and this misinterpretation can be seen as a symbol. Dong Qichang concluded this process with his words: "the way of painting lies in the universe and what we see before us (sheng ji or "vitality")".

Sheng ji is the embodiment of "spirit-lifting" and qi yun ("artistic conception"). Sheng ji is the status of painting and the painter. From this time on, the Chinese landscape paintings have moved into a free state that allows the painters to paint whatever they like. And from this time on, all was accumulated over time has become the support from the history.

This is the fundamental factor for the landscape paintings to present its continuity of history. Continuity of history means that the paintings are convergent in terms of the space but divergent in terms of the brushes. In other words, ink and colors that are based on "spirit-lifting" not only formed the landscape painting but also its history. As a result, the history of the landscape painting is "continuous" with respect to the time and it is "inclusive" in space.

When Xiao devoted himself into the history by "imitating", the history represented itself as an abundant oasis.

In this oasis of history, Xiao followed his

heart and grasped the roundness and smoothness of his work.

From Xiao's perspective, the roundness and smoothness is the concrete representation of the traditional landscape paintings, in which the spirit of the Mother Nature lies. Xiao has been working hard to search for the spirit of the Mother Nature in landscapes. His efforts are like a symphony of Nature that is playing behind the paintings.

Xiao's landscape paintings are simple. We can nothing else but waterfalls, stones, forests, fog and clouds. Such a pure and single image is similar to a fugue that guide us to reflect and stay away from all the troubles.

The landscape painting: the existence that faces the Nature. - in perfect sympathy with one another, with matching temperaments and perfect clarity both on and below the surface.

What is present here is the "material painting", the people at a certain point of time, and the landscape that transcended the boundary of time and space. When a painting exists in such ways, the human being is the hearts of the forests and waterfalls, and the landscape lies in his heart. This realizes the idea of "human being and the heaven become 'one'". The "one" is so concrete yet so "illusive". And it is in the philosophy of either Laozi or Heraclitus that these difficult ideas can be understood.

This is the tradition, the tradition of landscapes, of poems about the landscape and of the landscape paintings. When Confucius stood at the riverbank and sighed, we see this tradition. When Dante and Francesco Petrarch climbed the mountain or took a walk beside the river, we see this tradition.

Xiao did not make such statements in words. But, from his paintings, we know that he not only understands the tradition well, he also owns it.

When the painter realizes the fundamentals of art through techniques, they enter a new world with freedom. They can do whatever they like, and the only thing that confines him is his heart and personality.

The classic procedure or form is the revelation of heart and personality made by predecessors with the support of tradition. Xiao includes the tradition in his imitation of the classic masterpieces. He owns the tradition in his "hand-talks" with the predecessors and further reveal his true heart and personality also with the support of tradition.

Therefore, in Xiao's creation, we see how he is supported by the long tradition and how this helped him create a world full of roundness and smoothness in his paintings of mountains, rivers and forests when all the afore-mentioned contexts are blurred and invaded.

Paint brush and ink are the medium of traditions. Therefore, the support of tradition can best be symbolized with paint brush and ink. In his preface to an art book of landscape painting (1995), Xiao once wrote a short passage to reflect on the process of his creation: "I used to paint in a free and careless way. Those we support me would say that I painted what I wanted to paint with a free spirit. In fact, I knew that I had fallen into the trap of the old Yang-Zhou school of painting and lost my own way of creation. Although my free spirit was conveyed in the painting, there was nothing unique in it. From my observation of paintings by the predecessors, I learned that they took so much time thinking how to paint. They did not paint so frequently. This realization helped me to move away from my old habit and follow the traditional ways of painting. I did not understand what a paint brush and ink meant until I had communicated with the tradition for several years. Looking back at my past work and the paintings we see nowadays, most of them have not followed the tradition of the Chinese paintings. Bearing this in mind, I created my own way that followed the tradition. And I created the Mother Nature in my paintings with the magic of paint brush and ink." "Following the tradition" means that Xiao actually excluded the landscape paintings from the natural landscapes. And he categorized the interferences that are not about the fundamental implications of the landscape, such as "meaning", "value" and "function", into the nature of the landscapes. "I did not understand what a paint brush and ink meant until..." means that Xiao started to create a "new body" of the Mother Nature after he realized the magic of the paint brush and ink.

Frankly speaking, Xiao's brushes have transformed from being wild to being conservative. While he grasps the free spirit of Shi Tao and Ba Da Shan Ren, he also learns from other famous painters throughout the history. On the basis of streamlined brushes, he maintains a round and smooth style.

As for the use of ink, Xiao learned the essence of it from the way Huang Bing-Hong used the ink and thus his landscape paintings were once considered to be in the "dark tone" period. The paintings of this period are profound and grand, yet lack of elegance and smoothness. Due to Huang's enlightenment and his knowledge about the history of painting, Xiao went back to the history to search for evidences. Under the principles of "if you use black ink properly, you have no need for any other colors", he realized that the "black color" of the ink painting has its own unique and profound implication.

Paint brush and ink cannot be separated. Paint brush is the ink and ink is the paint brush. All techniques use the ink and paint brush to lay the foundation of the arrangement of the subjects and thus give the painting its own uniqueness. This is the key to the "spirit-lifting" of landscape paintings. If the painter pays too much attention to the truthful depiction of the appearance of subjects, he will be confined by the subjects and become what the "old Chinese language context" calls "the magician of painting" or "a paint master". The subject of landscape paintings is, of course, the mountains, rivers and forests. But such paintings also reveal the thoughts and personality of the painter. How he conveys these elements into the mountains, rivers and forests onto the piece of paper equals, in theory, to how he uses the paint brush and ink to depict the subjects. From the perspective of the techniques, the painter should highlight the uniqueness of the mind and soul with the images of these special qualities. The difference of the appearance of the subject should not be the first priority. This is the meaning of "new" of the "new body" proposed by Xiao. And the "object" in the sentence "now I know what

objects the paint brush and ink are" is represented here.
Based on that, we have obtained the possibility to research on the arrangement of subjects of the painting.

For a painter, the arrangement of the subjects of the painting is the final result of the creation, but the first impression for the viewer. Xiao's paintings always reveal an air of grandeur. All the subjects are magnificent, lively and full of vigor. And the viewers feel that the pressure comes from all angles. On the other hand, in the smaller paintings, we can also feel the power and pressure of Xiao's work. In other words, Xiao, with his work of art, has proven that the magnificence and power of a painting is not necessarily related to the size of the frame. Rather, the magnificence and power are both determined by the personality and perspective of the painter. Another perspective also proves that the landscape painting is not only a representation of the mountains, rivers and forests, it is also an expression of the painter's personality.

In Xiao's view, the depiction of the image or the arrangement of the subject should comply with the "three remoteness" principle: the remoteness of the horizon, the remoteness of the height and the remoteness of the depth. This principle sounds a little vague and too general, and it is certainly not so scientific. However, these disadvantages correspond to the characteristics of the "personality" of the painter. It is just like that most precise, human and "scientific" mathematics is the "fuzzy mathematics". In this way, Xiao is given freedom and a free spirit to create the Nature by following the inner voices.

Certainly, the "roundness" and "smoothness" cannot be covered simply with the word "magnificent". The roundness and smoothness that we see in Xiao's paintings are created by the paint brush and ink. As Xiao was once a jade sculptor and was recognized as the master of art at the national level, most viewers are keen to look for the reason of the roundness and smoothness from his earlier experience in art. It is not doubt that the experience of life, especially of the art, will somehow be revealed in the later stages of the creation in one way or another. However, the quality of Xiao's paintings is not transplanted from his experience in sculpting. It is constructed by the roundness and quality of the paint brush and ink that he uses. The direct visual experience tells us: the form of Xiao's painting does not follow the effects of the perspective skills. He even rejects or gives up this idea. The reason is that in the piling mountains and stones, the structural logic of the images are nearly "two-dimensional". This characteristic can be more appropriately analyzed with the modern ideas of the "structure". Moreover, we can see this universal phenomenon in the paintings of Wang Yuanqi (of the old Chinese language context) or the paintings of Paul C_zanne (of the "phonetic" context).

If we really want to find out how Xiao's paintings are influenced or impacted by his earlier experiences in jade sculptures, we believe that the answer can be found by looking at how he uses colors. The way he uses colors is deeply influenced by the tenderness, elegance and smoothness of jade. And it is for this very reason that Xiao's paintings usually reveal an air of tenderness no matter how magnificent they are. Jade is hard and strong in terms of the material, and warm and smooth in terms of the feeling it reveals. In other words, the jade combines the strong and the soft sides in one single piece of rock. From this characteristic of the jade, Xiao concretely realized the "dialectique" of art and his realization was confirmed by the history of landscape paintings. The meaning of "simplicity" is "secrecy", while the meaning of "complication" is "looseness". The meaning of "old" is "elegance", whereas the meaning of "young" is "green". Therefore, it is not enough (and at the same time, superficial) to explain the beauty of the dark yet elegant atmosphere of Xiao's paintings by the analysis of techniques. With such a special quality the combines the strong and the soft, and the giant mountains and rivers, Xiao is able to express his true personality. We can say that without the inspiration of colors, Xiao would not have been able to convey such strong power, profoundness, vigor and vitality in his paintings.

"Personality" is a clear reflection of the "natural landscape". Therefore, the images are free, natural and not confined in any way. If we can give up the division of the new and the old by time periods and use the non-historical ways of deconstruction that determine the vitality by the theory of evolution, we can really remove all kinds of barriers and appreciate the work of art in the traditional way with the supports from the tradition. By then, criteria and standards for evaluation and criticism will emerge and we will be able to immerse ourselves in the world full of work of art from all time periods. When the history becomes a "back-up" resource with no other pre-determinant or conditions attached, we are given our freedom, the freedom that belongs to this very moment only. All time periods, whether in Eastern or Western civilizations, co-exist without their time period being clearly marked. This is the mind of the tradition and the spirit of the landscapes.

"What is the landscape painting?" - If the landscape painting or the Chinese painting is like what we think they are, they will be trapped in difficulties in the past one or several centuries. However, such kind of difficulties will be looked into from a new perspective by asking this question.

"What is the landscape painting?" - If this is a question of painting that Xiao insists on contemplating by painting, his thought of the magnificent and beautiful world of the landscapes has clarified the "what" of the question in a positive way.

當代海上書畫生態的有效樣本——蕭海春的創作與海上特質的聯繫

文◎胡懿勳

南京東南大學藝術學系博士候選人

一、 前言

1991年10月深圳舉行「首屆中國當代名家字畫精品拍賣會」揭開了大陸地區書畫作品步入藝術品次級交易市場的序幕，繼而北京、上海都舉辦了類似的書畫作品拍賣，也取得了不錯的成績。大陸評論者認為這是「社會主義文化經濟市場建設過程」，透過國際通行的藝術品交易方式，使得大陸逐漸建立藝術品交易的市場規模。經過幾年發展之後，大陸藝術觀察者認為1997年藝術品拍賣業陷入困境，這是指當代藝術家的作品在拍會上的成交率與明清畫家作品產生明顯的差距，在收藏家以明清繪畫為主力蒐藏目標的強烈意識之下，當代藝術的作品拍賣會成交紀錄便乏善可陳了。然而，隨著明清畫家作品的成交熱絡，清代海上畫派成為拍賣市場的蒐藏焦點，而其海派畫家作品的時間範圍一直延續到民國時期，以及當代在上海活動的畫家作品。

另一個是從地域發展的因素，隨著經濟與商業開展進程，上海在清代成為近代中國藝術商品化最成功的範例，民國時期的十里洋場，1949年之後致力國際化的都市，大陸改革開放政策典範等種種因素，二十世紀末開始興起的藝術市場，近兩年已經成為，上海拍賣市場可堪與北京成為南北抗衡的趨勢。越來越細緻的觀察與討論，使我們對於上海書畫藝術的觀察，必須將目光集中在藝術市場與藝術生態的關係。

蕭海春作品十年前即隨台灣藝術市場的成熟與過激發展進入私人畫廊，可說是較早受到台灣書畫藏家熟悉的畫家，隨著兩岸藝術市場因體質差異發展兩種不同脈絡，蕭海春既在台灣市場受到檢驗，也在近年上海書畫市場有顯著的成績，從他的作品在上海書畫市場的接受度觀察，可以歸納出當代海上畫壇某些歷史與時代聯繫的軌跡。

蕭海春的書畫作品可能只是個例，但是從他不同風格、題材的作品中，又可以看到歷史的延續以及在當代上海書畫生態發展中特性，既有大環境因素的影響，也隨著當代藝術環境而波動；蕭海春的書畫作品可以作為對當代上海書畫生態的有效樣本。

二、 當代上海的繪畫生態與市場

清末以來至現代，中國書畫的地域性發展以五大畫派為主軸(1)，而京津畫派與海上畫派又是五大畫派之中的翹楚，居幾個地區的領導地位，往往在某些時期也代表了當時的繪畫主流，並引領著主流的繪畫思想。京津畫派主要指北京和天津地區的畫家。在清代沿襲正統派的畫學思想，以清代「四王」的繪畫思想為代表，強調繼承古法的重要。在民國時期的代表畫家有金城、陳師曾、齊白石、蔣兆和、溥儒、劉奎齡、胡佩衡、陳半丁、陳少梅、江采白、姚茫父、王夢白、湯定之、王雪濤、董壽平、李苦禪、周懷民、吳作人等，雖不直接追尋四王風格，各有自我風格表現，但強調傳統的思想，仍與四王的正統畫學有所聯繫。1949年後的代表畫家有李可染、白雪石、田世光、啓功、孫其峰、崔子范、俞致貞、賈又福、劉力上、楊延文等人，他們畫風轉爲與當時代的政治、社會風向緊密聯繫，有在筆墨上探求新的表現，脫離清初正統的樣貌，卻也因爲居全中國的政治中心，佔據最有利的發言舞台，他們的畫風也成爲一時爭相追隨的目標。不同的是，民國初年的北京畫派(或稱津京畫派)，與其說在筆墨上有所創新與突破，不如說，在畫學、書學、文藝思想上有長足的影響。

比之於京津畫派，海上派的發展從清代開始以商業化的成功，直至當代雖經過民國時期政商合一，社會劇烈轉型，到近二十年完全成爲衣個國際都會，依然秉持在商品化作基礎發展書畫藝術的態勢，而沒有太多的改變。北京畫壇依然把持著言論、思潮的發言權，而上海地區的書畫家則默默地將他們作品透過市場機制向全國，甚至全世界。尤其是在大陸近十年藝術市場興起之後，上海畫壇與京津畫壇儼然成爲南北兩個典型的代表，讓所有評論者的目光集中在這兩處地區；若要談論大陸前衛、最新的藝術潮流必須從北京談起；若要觀察藝術品的市場機制則需要以上海爲中心，擴及與其有關的江浙、廣東地區市場變化。

從近兩年的成交記錄可以看出，陸儼少、吳湖帆、吳昌碩、任熊、任伯年、謝稚柳等大名家，平均一材成交價超過約八萬元新台幣(2)，在拍賣市場仍然佔有絕對優勢，是延續上個世紀兩岸拍賣市場的書畫蒐藏主力目標。民國時期及已經有所成就的陸抑非、劉旦宅、唐雲、程十發、江寒汀等畫家，平均一材成交價超過四萬元新台幣，是上海拍賣市場的第二蒐藏目標。若是第二蒐藏目標以外畫家的作品，也會出現如主力目標一般高的成交行情；這種現象似乎無法以單純的藝術價值說明成交行情的超高現象。上海朵雲軒2003年秋拍會推出的近代倪田摹任熊《大梅詩意冊》設色紙本(26.5×32.5cm)，預估價爲45萬至85萬元人民幣，成交價高達880萬元人民幣。上海敬華拍賣公司今年春拍會推出的「海派書畫藝術」專題拍賣會，其中陶冷月僅一尺大的《柳夜孤舟》鏡屏，預估價2.8萬到3.8萬元，結果成交價達8.14萬元，創新了單尺拍賣成交最高紀錄。這兩個例子幾乎與十餘年前香港書畫拍賣市場將嶺南畫家及蘇仁山等廣東籍畫家作品行情炒出天價行情一般，現代與上海有淵源的畫家成爲另一波「以價制量」或「以價哄量」的籌碼；這些跡象顯示藏家手中必定擁有相當數量的海上名家作品，透過拍賣的競標，造成抬高一件作品行情，未出手的其他作品跟隨升值的目的。

根據歷年拍賣會成交行情分析，吳湖帆、吳昌碩、陸儼少、謝稚柳等人的書畫作品仍然逐漸升溫；較晚的前輩畫家劉旦宅以及賀天健、陶冷月、袁松年、韓敏、吳青霞、吳琴木、錢瘦鐵、應野平、關良、陳佩秋、謝之光、鄭午昌、鄭慕康、張大壯等人的作品行情似乎也還有升值的空間。這些海上畫家的行情在經過幾年一度港台兩地低迷的市場消沉，又在上海再度活躍起來。

相較書畫拍賣市場，屬於初級市場的畫廊業在上海卻面臨發展的困境(3)。有關統計資料表明，當一個地區每人國內生產毛額(GDP)達到8000美金才能形成對藝術品的社會性投資，而當GDP達到10000美金，才能形成完整、系統的藝術市場。上海現在的GDP只有4500美金卻有著傲視兩岸的熱烈程度，與台灣十年前的初級市場比較，有過之無不及，台灣十年前早以達到發達國家水準。據不完全統計，上海共有畫廊一千多家，其中80%以上是私人畫廊，而從事相關書畫買賣的人約有五萬人之譜(4)，上海私人畫廊正是由經濟發展的刺激所催生，興起以後卻無法被現存的藝術消費能力所承接。上海大環境處在現實的GDP4500美金和理論上認爲的理想市場GDP8000美金之間的大差距地帶，畫廊生存之艱難可見一斑。根據較有規模的私人專業畫廊業者表示，目前在上海普遍藝術消費者所可以接受的畫價在新台幣二千元至八千元之間，是銷售的主力價位，超過四萬元台幣價位則很難讓藝術消費者接受(5)。

三、 蕭海春繪畫特質與海上畫派的聯繫

從上海書畫拍賣和初級市場的差異分析，在初級市場成功的畫家往往也成爲次級市場的搶手目標，在初級市場上可以看到更多的風格與面貌，具有專業性的商業畫廊往往是進入次級市場的踏腳石，甚至於重疊性過高，也是初級市場經營困難的原因之一。其原因之二，是初級市場的區隔性不明顯，商業畫廊對自己的定位不準確，造成藝術消費者視聽混淆。由此，我們可以說，具有代表性的當代上海畫家，多數出現在次級市場造成交紀錄與行情，而不是初級市場長期經營的結果，他們往往是在次級市場成功之後，再進入初級市場，是一種逆向操作的模式，大大的不同於國際間的慣性模式。換句話說，當代上海畫家必須藉用清代海上派大家的成名方法，才能成就自己的自己的專業地位，清代海上名家以強勢之姿傲視拍賣會，而當代在上海活動的畫家，想要擠身海上之林，也要透過拍賣會，而不是先在初級市場接受時間考驗。

我們所得到的結論是，可以劃入當代海上之林的書畫家，均具有拍賣會行情，他們遠遠跳出了上海私人畫廊良莠不齊的泥淖；當他們在次級市場受到肯定之後，才會回頭選擇進入初級市場累積基礎。根據這個結論進一步論述，拍賣會上成交的書畫作品，從清代到當代有順序地、集中地顯現了海上畫家的繪畫風格，也成爲觀察者、

評論者歸納分析的有效樣本。

丁羲元先生在《收藏家》發表的文章中指明，海上派具備以下四項特質：

（一）首先，海派充溢著時代氣息和愛國精神，是其顯著的特點。海派形成及發展的歷史是中國社會制度劇烈變化的時代，是近代歷史上最爲動蕩的歲月。

（二）其次，海派繼承並發展了我國繪畫的優秀傳統。形成了以花鳥畫和人物畫_主體，以大寫意畫和金石風爲發展潮流的藝術特點。

（三）第三，海派在對西畫藝術及其技法的借鑒、吸收和融會上有力地推進了中國繪畫的發展。因_海派是依存於近代國際都會上海的崛起和發展，因此在對外繪畫交流上海派有著眞正意義上不同於歷史上任何時期和畫派的交流時空。

（四）第四，海派名家大多來自社會下層，與民間藝術有著天然的聯繫，他們的繪畫，從內容至形式，都吸取了民間藝術之長而加以提高，因而能達到雅俗共賞。

就這四點而論，當代上海的畫家也延續歷史的傳承關係，在歷史累積的基礎上繼續首先，發展自己的繪畫風格。大陸畫家雖然紛紛自覺地走進藝術市場尋求自己的專業定位，對於愛國精神與民族風格依然常掛嘴邊。其次，即使現代水墨結合抽象的、表現的、複合媒材等等形式，僅在表現媒材具有傳統意義，但是許多秉持傳統水墨的畫家還是在國際都會的上海受到歡迎。第三，當代書畫畫家開宗明義，理所當然地運用西畫的理念、技巧、創作觀，也未自認會發生消化不良的現象。最後，打破畫家身分在藝術社會的傳統定位，雅俗的觀點轉而爲由市場機制來決定。

蕭海春的繪畫1993年出現在台北忠孝東路阿波羅大廈裡的私人畫廊，正值台灣藝術市場蓬勃發展的時期，也是台灣現代水墨畫壇熱烈討論，中國水墨畫何去何從，或者面臨消亡的關頭。台灣藝術市場蓬勃使得一批書畫家依靠著數量可觀的成交記錄，和逐年高漲的成交行情，成爲藝術圈的佼佼者；知名度的提高，作品在市場的成功行銷，也形成書畫的主流風格。蕭海春的繪畫出現在台北也隱約的牽連著這兩個議題。他幾種不同風格的作品，有傳統青綠山水風格，近代濃重墨韻的黃賓虹畫風，以及類近倪雲林山水的淡雅，加上具有個人特色，以寫生爲基礎的現代水墨畫風格，可以說包括了傳統與現代的延續與開展，尤其是他深厚的傳統基礎，以及有意追隨唐宋大家的繪畫風格，引起台灣藏家的注意，更深刻的爲水墨畫何去何從寫下具體的意見。

蕭海春的作品近年在上海拍賣會及畫廊界均佔有重要的地位，他多樣性的風格大多與古代傳統有著深厚的淵源，既是擺脫了「現代與傳統」論戰的多餘，也反應了大陸藏家對於海上的品味，多少還是循著清代的老味道。他在一九八〇年代的人物畫獲得許多榮譽，筆下的李白、八大山人取法寫意卻不失寫實造形的意象，可以說是清代海派的傳統。儘管蕭海春不乏花鳥、人物題材作品，山水畫應該才具有代表性。在山水畫上蕭海春毫不諱言地向古人致上最尊敬的意思；從礬頭皴裡探索五代巨然的筆意；在折帶皴石與枯木法效倪雲林；龔賢、石濤、八大、齊白石的筆意筆法均在蕭海春的探求之列。脫離黃賓虹的重墨山水之後，蕭海春更加自由地從實地寫生中發展山水，這種風格與動機是大陸自李可染以來大環境的影響，卻也成爲作爲海上畫家的蕭海春，具有現代性的標誌(6)。

就畫家的社會身分而言，清代海上畫家具有劃時代的特質，也與民國初年北京畫壇以知識份子爲首的情況有所不同。清代海上畫家離開傳統士族階層的高姿態，許多從民間出身的畫家在贊助者的支持之下，不但在上海立足更在畫壇揚名立萬，因此，從滿清帝制過渡到以西方民主爲基礎的政體，上海書畫界的現代化並未受到阻擾。蕭海春一九六四年在玉雕廠工作的經歷，符合了海上畫家就民間藝術與書畫交流的海上特質，由於時空條件的轉變，蕭海春在較爲健全的藝術市場上接觸更寬廣的藝術消費者，而非是清代特定階層藝術贊助者，更加有利於他的書畫作品的開拓。蕭海春不因爲具有玉雕廠工作經歷而被劃入民間書畫工作者之列，在講求行銷策略和作品銷售的實戰環境中，蕭海春在上海能夠脫穎而出，甚至走出上海，在港台地區也有佳績，實爲不易。

四、結語

關於水墨畫存亡和何去何從的議題，似乎近年已經淡去，然在十年前由兩岸畫家共構的台灣藝術市場的事實，說明了現代書畫創作與其高談闊論的建築一些不切實際的論述，還不如在發展的事實中尋找眞實的面貌。作爲觀察當代上海畫壇的有效樣本，蕭海春的作品似乎與過去聯繫緊密，符合了普遍藝術消費市場的品味，他也有自己的風格面貌，吸引了會看門道的藏家進行系列蒐藏。透過大陸由於骨董文物、古代書畫的爭購，以及官方介入的因素，而特別發達的次級市場，以及因爲體制不全而營運艱難的初級市場，蕭海春可說是兩面得意，加上近年網路行銷藝術品的熱絡，蕭海春的經紀人、代理商更企圖將他推上國際。

蕭海春在作品表現和創作歷程均可成爲有效樣本。他的作品在市場的成功行銷是當代上海書畫生態的專業取向標本，他個人的努力以及創作的多樣性在上海獲得高程度的接受，表明上海藝術消費層次具有明顯的區隔，資深藏家的愛好與一般市民階層的品味，顯然在蕭海春這裡得到一道明顯的界線。我們也從畫商對蕭海春的行銷過程歸納，上海藝術市場的兩級化仍然混沌不明，更大範圍而論，大陸藝術市場的特質也從有效樣本的檢證中獲得證實。至於更多地區、更大範圍的比較申論工作，當在獲取更多具有代表性樣本之後，可以繼續進行的工作。

1 五大畫派指，京津畫派、海上畫派、嶺南畫派、長安畫派及金陵畫派。其形成以地域為範圍，有歷史傳統脈絡可以依循的海上畫派、金陵畫派於清初至清末即已成熟並有所延續，津京畫派與嶺南畫派形成於清末民初，長安畫派則最晚，約於1949年之後形成。

2 依照上海拍賣會行情為單尺二萬元人民幣，台灣藝術市場交易習慣以「材」為計價單位，大陸則以「尺」為計價單位，兩者均約為三十公分左右。

3 一般而論，國際間藝術市場分為初級市場及次級市場，初級市場指如私人商業畫廊，可直接銷售其所代理、經紀的畫家作品；次級市場指拍賣會等經過競標銷售的交易市場。初級與次級市場加上評論者、學校、政府機構等中介機制三者形成密切互動關係，構成完整藝術市場機制與規模。

4 上海多數號稱畫廊的店舖，往往以經營畫框裝裱為主的項目，因此，就專業性而言十分不足，也反映了台灣二十年前藝術市場的初步階段景象。所謂從事藝術品買賣，是指「跑單幫」之流，以個人轉賣仿作、仿古董的各種藝術社會邊緣的人。

5 根據上海私人畫廊業界的說法，銷路好的水墨畫在八千元新台幣以內，油畫則在一萬六千元新台幣以內。

6 以實地寫生轉換為繪畫內容的表現，是大陸地區水墨畫大區域、大面積的影響，在北京、廣東也有同樣表現。

"Effective Specimens" from Contemporary Shanghai's Artistic Ecosystem:

The Works of Xiao Haichun and the Unique Traits of the Shanghai School

Hu Yixun
University of Dongnan, Nanjing, Ph. D Candidute

Introduction

The "Premier Public Auction of Renowned Works of Contemporary Chinese Calligraphy and Painting," held in Shenzhen in October of 1991 heralded the gradual entry of Mainland art into the secondary art trading market. Similar art auctions held in Beijing and Shanghai all ended up being enormously successful. Mainland commentators described this as part of "the process of socialist cultural and economic market development:" the gradual establishment of the Mainland art market through exchanges with the international art trading community. However, after only a few years of development, the Mainland art auction industry had entered a tough period in 1997: at auctions, the works of modern artists were not selling as much as the works of Ming and Qing Dynasty artists. With collectors focusing their main attention on the works of Ming and Qing era paintings, there was not much good news to be heard on the sales of contemporary artists' works. Yet with the elevated sales of Ming and Qing Dynasty works, works by artists of the Qing era's Shanghai school of painting became hot items for collectors on the auction market. Eventually, these collector's interest in the Shanghai school of painting expanded from the works of the Qing era all the way into the Shanghai school of the Republican Period, and even grew to encompass the works of contemporary Shanghai painters.

A factor for consideration when analyzing Chinese painting is its regional development. In the midst of economic and commercial growth during the Qing Dynasty, Shanghai's art scene came to stand out as the single most successful example of commercialized art in modern China. With the Bund of the Republican Period, the city's role as the center of the drive for internationalization after 1949, and its status as a model of the Mainland's opening and reform policy, along with a number of other factors, Shanghai's environment has caused the Chinese art market, which just started gaining strength towards the end of the Twentieth Century, to begin to show a trend of regional polarization over the last two years: with Shanghai's auction market in the South striking a balance with Beijing's auction market in the North. In order to more carefully and thoroughly observe and discuss Shanghai art, we must focus our attention on the connections between Shanghai's art market and its artistic environment.

Ten years ago, as the Taiwan art market developed to maturity, Xiao Haichun's works entered personal collections in Taipei. You could say that Xiao caught the eye of Taiwanese collectors very early on, and while the art markets on the two sides of the Taiwan Strait continue to develop in different directions on account of systematic differences, Xiao Haichun has not only received affirmation on the Taiwanese market, but has also enjoyed prominent success in recent years in the Shanghai art market. In analyzing his success on the Shanghai art market, one can find the traces of connections with the history of Shanghai painting and with Shanghai's contemporary environment.

The works of Xiao Haichun may be just one specimen, but from his various different styles and themes, one can see development upon the basis of historical traditions, as well as the unique traits of an artist cultivated in contemporary Shanghai's artistic environment. Not only are a number of larger environmental influences present in his work, various transformations resulting from the contemporary artistic environment are apparent. All of this just goes to show that the works of Xiao Haichun could serve as effective specimens of the artistic ecosystem of contemporary Shanghai.

The Artistic Environment and Art Market in Contemporary Shanghai

The regional development of Chinese art from the late Qing Dynasty through to the present has revolved primarily around five major regional schools of painting (1), led by the Beijing-Tianjin School and the Shanghai School. Cities' or regions' leading positions have also made them the leaders of mainstream styles and artistic thought in certain eras. The Beijing-Tianjin School mainly refers to painters in the Beijing and Tianjin region. In the Qing Dynasty, this school followed the artistic thought of the Orthodox School, represented by the painting ideology of the "Four Wang's" of the Qing era, which emphasized the importance of continuing ancient painting methods. Some painters active in this school during the Republican era include Jin Cheng, Chen Shizong, Qi Baishi, Jiang Yaohe, Fu Ru, Liu Kuiling, Hu Peiheng, Chen Banding, Chen Shaomei, Jiang Caibai, Yao Mangfu, Wang Mengbai, Tang Dingzhi, Wang Xuetao, Yun Shouping, Li Kuchan, Zhou Huaimin, Wu Zuoren, and various others. While they each had their own painting styles and did not seek to directly copy the styles of the "Four Wang's," they emphasized traditional painting philosophies, and remained closely linked to the "Four Wang's" Orthodox school of painting. Some painters active in this school in the post-1949 era include Li Keran, Bai Xueshi, Tian Shiguang, Qi Gong, Sun Qifeng, Cui Zifan, Yu Zhizhen, Jia Youfu, Liu Lishang, Yang Yanwen, and others. Changes of direction in many of these painters' styles were intimately interlinked with changes in the political and social currents of modern China. Some sought out new forms of expression using their brush and ink, breaking away from the orthodox styles of the early Qing; and with their location in the political heart of China, they clearly held the ideal stage to make their voice and ideas heard, causing their painting styles to become leading examples followed by many other painters. What is unique is that the innovations and breakthroughs of the Beijing School of Painting (otherwise known as the Beijing-Tianjin School of Painting) of the early years of the Republican Period in terms of ink painting, were not as strong as their long-term extensive influence on painting, calligraphy, and literary thought.

In contrast to the Beijing-Tianjin school of painting, the development of the Shanghai school of art has been constantly linked to commercialism. This trend stands out all the way from the initial successes of commercial art in the Qing Dynasty, through the integration of government and business in the Republican period, through the massive social transitions of the contemporary era, all the way through to Shanghai's development into an international city over the past 20 years. Through all of this, the Shanghai School has always held firm to its stance of developing the arts of calligraphy and painting on the basis of commercialism, with little change evident over the years. Nowadays, Beijing painting circles continue to serve as the nation's leading voice with regards to trends in popular thought, while artists in the Shanghai region quietly employ market mechanisms to spread their works outwards across the entire country and even the entire world. Shanghai and Beijing-Tianjin painting circles have been neatly divided into the model representatives of North and South, especially with the rebirth of the Mainland art market over the last ten years, bringing these two areas into critics' focus. Those who want to discuss avant-garde or the newest artistic trends on the Mainland need to place their focus on Beijing; while those who want to observe the market mechanisms governing the art trading industry will need to focus their attention on Shanghai, while also keeping a close eye on market developments in a wider area, including nearby Jiangsu, Zhejiang, and Guangdong provinces.

From records of transactions over the last two years, it is clear that a number of painters' works, including those of Lu Yanshao, Wu Hufan, Wu Changshuo, Ren Xiong, Ren Bonian, and Xie Zhiliu, usually sell for an average price of 80 thousand NTD or more(2). Works by these artists still hold the competitive advantage on the auction market, and continue, as they did in the last century, to serve as the chief focus of collectors on the auction market on both sides of the Taiwan Straits. A single piece from the more successful painters of the Republican Period, such as Lu Yifei, Liu Danzhai, Tang Yun, Cheng Shifa, and Jiang Hanting, will generally sell for more than 40 thousand NTD, making these artists' works the secondary focus of collectors on the Shanghai auction market. Furthermore, even works by artists that are outside of this second stratum could possibly sell for prices as high as that of the first stratum; it seems almost impossible to use pure artistic value to explain the phenomenon of high prices in this market. The modern artist Ni Tian's sketchbook imitation of Ren Xiong's Plum Album (26.5×32.5cm) was originally predicted to sell for a price somewhere between 450 thousand and 850 thousand RMB, when in reality it ended up selling at the Shanghai Duo Yun Xuan Autumn 2003 Art Works Auction for 8.8 million RMB. At the "Chinese Paintings of the Shanghai

School" theme auction held this spring by the Shanghai Jinghua Auction Company, Tao Lengyue's screen work A Solitary sailing which measures only one "chi" (translator's note: 1 chi= around one-third of a meter, or about one foot), was originally predicted to sell for a price somewhere between 28 and 38 thousand RMB, while its final selling price actually reached 81,400 RMB, setting an all new price record by unit size for a painting. These two examples are reminiscent of ten years ago on the Hong Kong auction market, when works by painters of the Lingnan school, as well as those of Su Renshan and other Guangdong painters sold for unnaturally high prices. The Shanghai painters of today have begun yet another wave of "creating quality on the basis of sales prices" or "raising quality through the basis of sales prices;" all signs indicate that quite a few collectors must have a decent amount of Shanghai painters' works in their hands, and that they hope to use auction attendees' bids to raise the value of these artists' works, so that other works not yet on sale will gain value and sell at elevated prices in the future.

According to an analysis of auction prices over the years, the sales prices of works by Wu Hufan, Wu Changshuo, Lu Yanshao, Xie Zhiliu and a number of other painters continue to slowly rise; while the sales prices of works by later painters such as Liu Danzhai, Jia Tianjian, Tao Lengyue, Yuan Songnian, Han Min, Wu Qingxia, Wu Qinmu, Qian Shoutie, Ying Shu-ping, Guan Liang, Chen Peiqiu, Xie Zhi-guang, Zhen Wuchang, Zhen Mukang, and Zhang DaZhuang seem to also have some room left to rise. Having made it through the drop in prices over the last few years in the turbid Hong Kong and Taiwan markets, these Shanghai painters' works have started seeing some action again in the Shanghai market.

Compared to the secondary auction market, art galleries in Shanghai's primary market face quite a few difficulties hindering their development(3). Relevant statistical data shows that a region's GDP should reach 8 thousand USD in order for a space for art investment to really start to take shape in society; the data also shows that it is not until a region's GDP reaches 10 thousand USD that a fully integrated, systematic art market can truly develop. Shanghai's current GDP is only 4500 USD, yet it already has one of the active art markets in the Greater China region. It is certainly no worse off than Taiwan's primary market ten years ago, when Taiwan had already, very early on, clearly attained the status of a developed country. According to incomplete statistics, Shanghai has over 1000 galleries, of which over 80% are private galleries, and around 50 thousand people involved in business related to calligraphy and painting auctions (4). The opening of Shanghai's numerous private galleries has been driven by the excitement of economic development, but these galleries are in fact out of sync with the consumer capacity present in the market. The giant gap between Shanghai's actual GDP of 4500 USD and the art market's theoretically ideal minimum GDP of 8 thousand USD illustrates just one of many difficulties faced by these private galleries. According to statements from fairly well-established individuals in the gallery industry, the prices that an average Shanghai consumer could accept at the moment would be between 2 thousand and 8 thousand NTD for a painting. Thus, this is the main price range on the market here today. Paintings with price tags exceeding the range of 40 thousand NTD were very unlikely to be accepted by consumers (5).

Unique Traits of Xiao Haichun's Paintings and their Links to the Shanghai School of Painting

In analyzing the differences between the Shanghai art auction market and the primary market, one notices that painters that obtain success in the primary market often see their works become hot items on the secondary market. One ends up seeing much greater diversity in styles and visions on the primary market, while specialized commercial galleries often serve as stepping-stones for artists to enter the secondary market. One of the main difficulties faced by management in the primary art market is simply the high degree of overlap that this market faces. Another source of difficulty is that the primary market is not clearly layered, and commercial galleries are unsure about their positioning in the market, leaving consumers confused. Due to these problems in the primary market, we see that the majority of contemporary Shanghai painters appear first in the secondary market, making sales and setting prices for their works, rather than earning their reputation as a result of long and hard work in the primary market. Most, in fact, do not enter the primary market until after attaining success in the secondary market, creating an inverse pattern far different from what is usually seen in the international market. In other words, one could say that contemporary Shanghai painters attain fame through the same methods as the Shanghai school of painting in the Qing era. In order to successfully establish their own professional status, famous Shanghai school painters of the Qing Dynasty set their sights high on the auctions of the time; while the painters that are currently active in present day Shanghai, in order to find their spot in the Shanghai market, have also chosen the course of establishing their reputations through auctions, rather than withstanding the conventional test of time in the primary market.

Our conclusion is that contemporary Shanghai artists who want to make it to the top usually work to earn their reputation at auctions, and have managed to avoid the confusion of Shanghai's private galleries; only after attaining affirmation on the secondary market do they choose to turn back and build up a base in the primary market. Following this conclusion just one step further, it would be reasonable to say that the artworks sold at Shanghai auctions, all the way from the Qing Dynasty through to the contemporary era, have, in an orderly and centralized manner, shown the representative painting styles of Shanghai artists, and have also served as effective samples for analysis by observers and commentators.

In an essay published in "Collector," Mr. Ding Xiyuan points out the following four distinct traits of the Shanghai school of painting:

The most notable trait of the Shanghai school is that it is brimming with the flavor of the times and a patriotic spirit. This painting school came into being and grew to maturity during an era of massive changes in Chinese society, a period widely regarded as one of the most turbulent in China's modern history.

Secondly, the Shanghai school inherited and developed China's outstanding painting traditions, forming a unique artistic style based in bird and flower painting and figure painting, while also developing along the lines of "Da-xie-yi"'s free-hand brushwork and the "Jin-shi" style of painting.

Third, the Shanghai School's ability to learn from, draw upon, and blend Western painting's styles and techniques has provided the development of Chinese painting with an effective boost. As the Shanghai school depends on the growth and development of the modern international city of Shanghai, these painters are located in a very different city and a very different era than that of any other school of Chinese painting throughout history, providing them with much more opportunities for international exchange.

Fourth, the majority of well-known painters of the Shanghai School originally came from lower social classes, giving them a natural connection to folk art. Their paintings, in terms of both content and form, have extracted the strong points of folk art and improved upon them, creating works that suit popular tastes as well as the refined tastes of connoisseurs.

These four points show that Shanghai's contemporary painters inherited historical traditions, while also managing to develop their own painting style on the basis of these traditions. While mainland painters consciously enter the art market one after another to seek out their own professional standing, they nonetheless continue to make constant references to patriotism and national styles. Secondly, while modern ink and wash painting integrates abstract visions, expressionism, mixed media, and various other forms, the only form with any remaining traditional significance is the use of expressionistic media. However, a number of painters who continue to strictly uphold these traditions of ink and wash painting are still welcome in the international city of Shanghai. Thirdly, contemporary painters and calligraphers employ ideas, techniques, and creative perspectives from Western painting in a manner that is both natural and direct, never showing any concern that such methods could result in what could be called "artistic indigestion." Finally, these painters have smashed the traditional methods by which painters attain their status, leaving status to be decided by market mechanisms rather than by critics.

Xiao Haichun's paintings first appeared in the private Apollo Art Gallery on Taipei's ChungXiao East Road in 1993. These works arrived not only at a moment of dynamic growth in the Taiwanese art market, but also at a time when Taiwanese ink and wash painting circles were passionately debating what course Chinese ink and wash painting should follow next, and whether or not it was approaching its death. The boom in the Taiwanese art market caused a number of artists to rely on considerable sales and annual increases in their works' market value to become standout figures in regional art circles; with the growth of their fame, and success on the market, they were also able to shape mainstream painting styles. The appearance of Xiao Haichun's paintings in Taipei was subtly related to these two features of the art market at the time. Xiao's works incorporate multiple different styles, including a traditional blue and green landscape style, a more modern style employing dense ink reminiscent of the paintings of Huang Binhong, a quietly elegant landscape style reminiscent of Ni Yunlin, along with his own individual style of modern ink wash painting based on real life sketches. With these many different styles, one could say that Xiao's works both inherited traditional methods and expanded upon them. It was his solid traditional base, along with his attempts to capture the styles of great painters of the Song and Tang Dynasty, that really caught the attention of Taiwanese collectors, as well as providing a clear possible direction for the future of ink and wash painting.

In recent years, the works of Xiao Haichun have occupied an important position in Shanghai's art auctions and gallery circles. The origins of a number of his styles can be seen in ancient traditional practices, and while managing to break away from the excessive controversy regarding "modernity and tradition," he has also reflected the fact that Mainland collectors' taste for paintings from the Shanghai school are still strongly based in its Qing era styles. Xiao's figure paintings from the 1980's have received a number of honors, with his portrayals of Li Bai and Pa-ta Shan-jen employing freehand brushwork without losing the imagery of realist painting: one could say that this is a tradition of the Qing era's Shanghai school. Whereas Xiao Haichun has a number of works that fit into the categories of bird and flower painting and figure painting, the painting style most representative of him and his talents would have to be landscape painting. In his landscape paintings, Xiao Haichun clearly and candidly shows his deep respect for the methods employed by traditional artists; exploring the style of Ju Ran of the Five Dynasties with his use of the wrinkle method to show fog and clouds at the peak of mountains; imitating the styles and techniques of Ni Yunlin in using the wrinkle method to show the lines and contours of rocks and withered trees; even the styles of Long Xian, Shi Tao, Ba Da, and Qi Baishi have all been part of his explorations. Breaking away from Huang Binhong's ink-heavy landscape painting style, Xiao Haichun was able to more freely develop his landscape painting style from his own spontaneous sketches. In this case, his style and motivations were influenced by the overall environment in painting circles that had been around since the appearance of Li Keran. And these methods ended up becoming a modernistic symbol of Xiao Haichun of the Shanghai school of painting, (6).

The Shanghai school of painters of the Qing era created a unique new way of thinking with regards to the social standing of painters, a way of thinking that in fact ended up defining their era. Even in contrast to the Beijing school of painting of the early Republican period, which was primarily composed of intellectuals, the Shanghai School of the Qing Dynasty left behind the traditional lofty stances of the scholarly class, and included a number of painters of rather humble origins. With help from their supporters, these painters were able to not only set themselves up in Shanghai, they even ended up making quite a name for themselves in painting circles far and wide. On account of this unique characteristic, the modernization and development of the Shanghai school of painting has never been blocked or experienced setbacks during the political transition from the imperial rule of the Manchurian Qing Dynasty system to the Republican system based in Western Democratic thought. In fact, Xiao Haichun's experience working in a jade carving factory in 1964 was in harmony with Shanghai painters' unique stance towards folk art and artistic exchange. With the passing of time, Xiao Haichun's ability to interact with a more diverse group of art buffs in a comparatively strong market, rather than simply enjoying the support of the social classes designated to appreciate art (as was the case during the Qing Dynasty), has been very beneficial to his pioneering spirit and the development of his artwork. It is not just because Xiao Haichun had experience working at a jade carving factory that he has been characterized as a popular folk artist, or artist of the people; in his sales and distribution strategies, Xiao Haichun has not only shown off his talents in Shanghai. He has also shown strong performance outside of Shanghai, in Taiwan and Hong Kong, which is a truly rare feat.

Conclusion

Discussions of the death of ink and wash painting and its future path seem to have quieted down over the past few years. And the reality of the Taiwan art market, built up by artists from both sides of the Taiwan Straits ten years ago, shows that it is better to seek out the truth in the actual course of development than to sit around thinking about some of the lofty, and often unrealistic and empty, debates of the modern art world. As valid specimens to analyze contemporary Shanghai art circles, the works of Xiao Haichun are apparently closely linked to the past, in keeping with the conventional tastes of the art market, while also demonstrating their own unique styles, attracting art collectors to purchase these works. One could say that Xiao Haichun should be proud of his accomplishments on the Mainland's secondary market, which is especially developed on account of the trade in antiques and ancient works of calligraphy and painting (let us also not forget the role of official intervention), as well as on its primary market, which faces a number of operational difficulties due to its incomplete organizational structure. And don't forget to add the sale of art works over the Internet, a process that has become popular in recent years, as we see Xiao Haichun's agents pushing for the spread of his works onto the international stage.

The representative and creative process behind Xiao Haichun's works make then effective specimens for analyzing Shanghai's contemporary artistic environment. His works' success on the market stands out as a specialized representative of the orientation of the contemporary Shanghai art scene. His individual endeavors and diverse creative strengths have been warmly welcomed in Shanghai, showing that he is able to capture the fancy of respected collectors as well as blend with the tastes of average city people, two levels of taste which are clearly separated in his works. Yet, we can also conclude, from the processes by which Xiao Haichun's works are sold and distributed by art dealers, that the Shanghai art market as a whole continues to lack clear and orderly stratification of these two distinct consumer groups. These particular traits of the Mainland art market can be confirmed on an even larger scale through the examination of such effective artistic specimens. As for the examination of other regions, or larger scale comparative analyses, these are things that will have to be done after more representative specimens are able to be collected.

1 The five schools of painting refers to the Beijing- Tianjin school, the Shanghai school, the Lingnan school, the Changan school, and the Chingling school. These schools developed on a regional basis. The Shanghai and Chingling schools, coming from regions with historical painting traditions that could be followed, had already developed into mature and stable schools in the era between the early and late Qing era. The Beijing- Tianjin school and the Lingnan school were formed between the later Qing Dynasty and the early Republican Period, while the Changan school was the latest, appearing after 1949.

2 According to prices at Shanghai auctions, the usual unit price of 1 "chi" is around RMB 20 thousand yuan. The unit "cai" is most commonly used to measure unit prices in the Taiwan art market, while "chi" is used to measure unit prices on the Mainland art market. Both units of measurement are equal to roughly 30 centrimeters.

3 Generally, the international art market is divided into two levels: the primary market and the secondary

market. The primary market refers to private commercial galleries that serve directly as agents to sell works of art; the secondary market refers to auctions and other trading markets where works are sold by bidding. The primary and secondary markets, together with critics, academic circles, government organizations and other third-person intermediary mechanisms come together in a close inter-dynamic relationship, forming an integrated art market.

4 In a situation reminiscent of the initial stages of development of the Taiwan art market twenty years ago, the majority of so-called "galleries" in Shanghai in fact deal primarily in the framing and mounting of paintings, and as a result lack the professional knowledge required of a gallery. The so-called "art trade" mainly refers to roaming traders, people on the fringe of society who re-sell copies of artworks, fake antiques, and various other types of art.

5 According to statements from figures in the private gallery trade in Shanghai, according to the market conditions in Shanghai, marketable ink and wash paintings should sell for 8 thousand NTD or less, while oil paintings should sell for 16 thousand NTD or less.

6 The practice of on-the-spot sketches serving as the backbone of paintings has been widely influential in Mainland ink and wash painting circles, and can also be seen in the works of artists from Beijing and Guangdong.

圖　版
PLATES

1993～1999

空山水流意

Quiet Stream in Deserted Mountain

1994

紙，設色，軸

Hanging scroll, ink and color on paper.

131.5x27.6cm

夜靜月映門

Moon-lit Gate in Quiet Night

1994

紙，設色，軸

Hanging scroll, ink and color on paper.

131.5x27.6cm

嵐光輕鎖翠

Field Half-covered in Mist

1994

紙，設色，軸

Hanging scroll, ink and color on paper.

131.5x27.6cm

山中含真意

The Essence of Mountains

1994

紙，設色，軸

Hanging scroll, ink and color on paper.

131.5x27.6cm

山中有真意
The Essence of Mountains

1995
紙，淺設色，軸
Hanging scroll, ink and light color on paper.
66x23.9cm

白雲怡悅

Contented Clouds: Spring

1996

紙，淺設色，軸

Hanging scroll, ink and light color on paper.

208x99cm

乙巳三月海

浮嵐暖翠

Mist-blanketed Field: Summer

1996

紙，淺設色，軸

Hanging scroll, ink and light color on paper.

208x99cm

霜林染秋
Dewy Forest Colored in Gold: Autumn

1997
紙，淺設色，軸
Hanging scroll, ink and light color on paper.
208x99cm

幽谷清冬

Secluded Valley in Winter

2004

紙，水墨，軸

Hanging scroll, ink on paper.

211x100.1cm

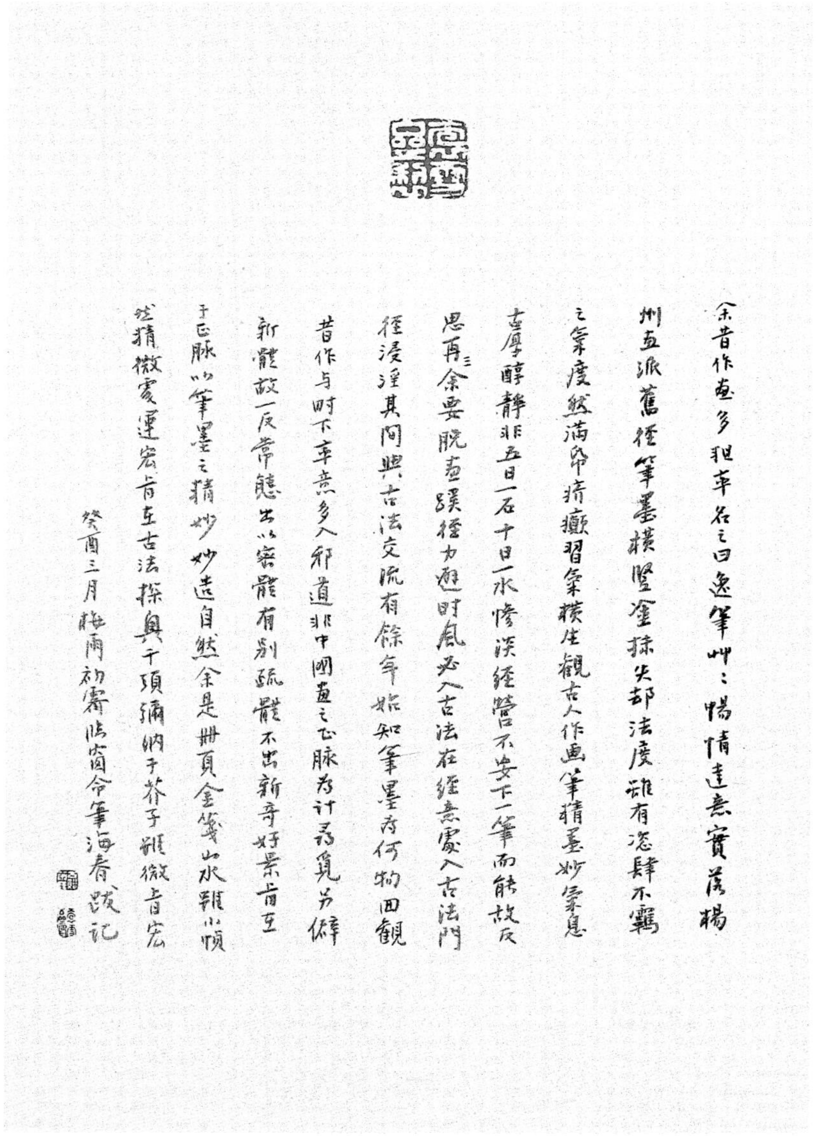

以小觀大冊

Mountain and River Scenery Series 1

1993

紙，書法，冊頁

Album leaf, calligraphy, ink on paper.

23x7.1cm

以小觀大冊

Mountain and River Scenery Series 2

1993

紙，水墨，冊頁

Album leaf, ink on paper.

23x7.1cm

以小觀大冊

Mountain and River Scenery Series 3

1993

紙，水墨，冊頁

Album leaf, ink on paper.

23x7.1cm

以小觀大冊

Mountain and River Scenery Series 4

1993

紙，水墨，冊頁

Album leaf, ink on paper.

23x7.1cm

以小觀大冊

Mountain and River Scenery Series 5

1993

紙，水墨，冊頁

Album leaf, ink on paper.

23x7.1cm

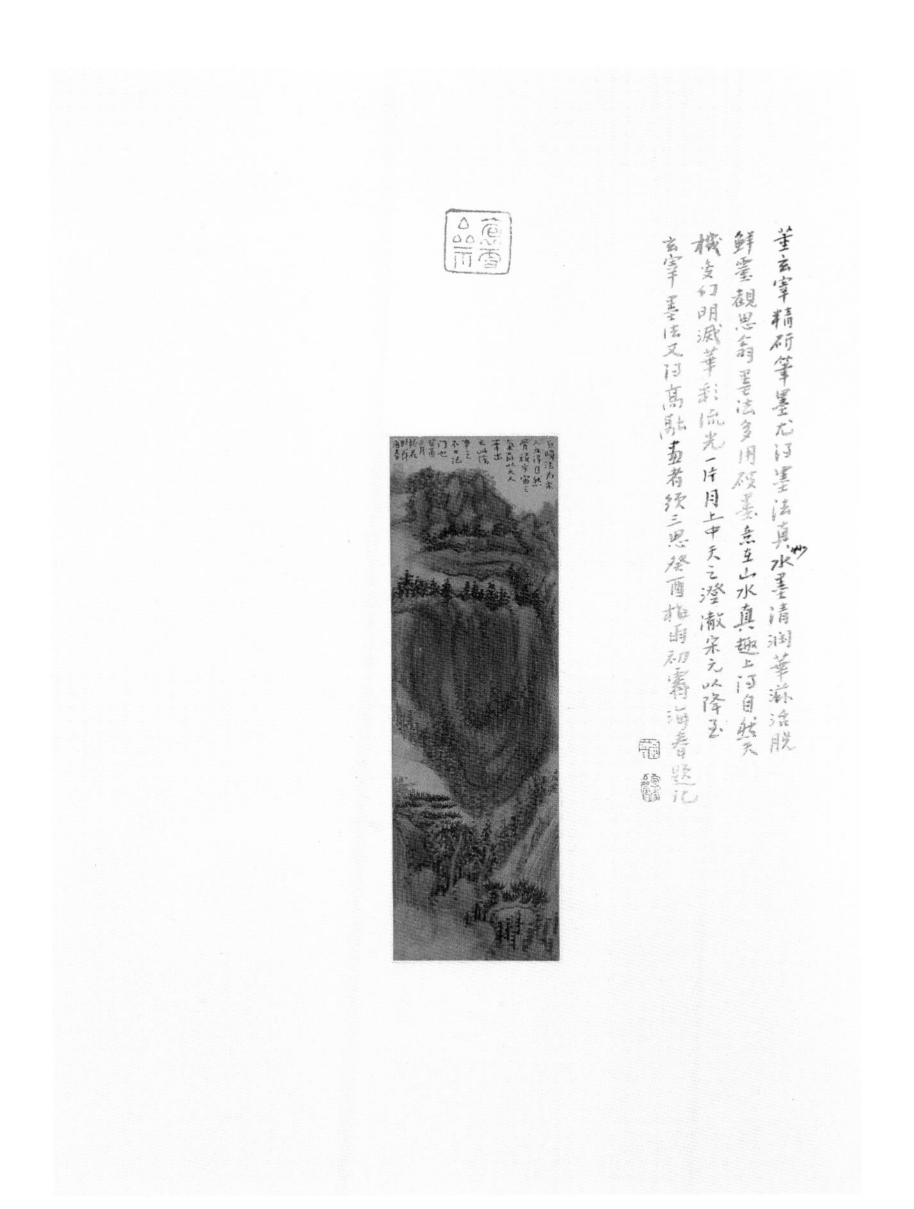

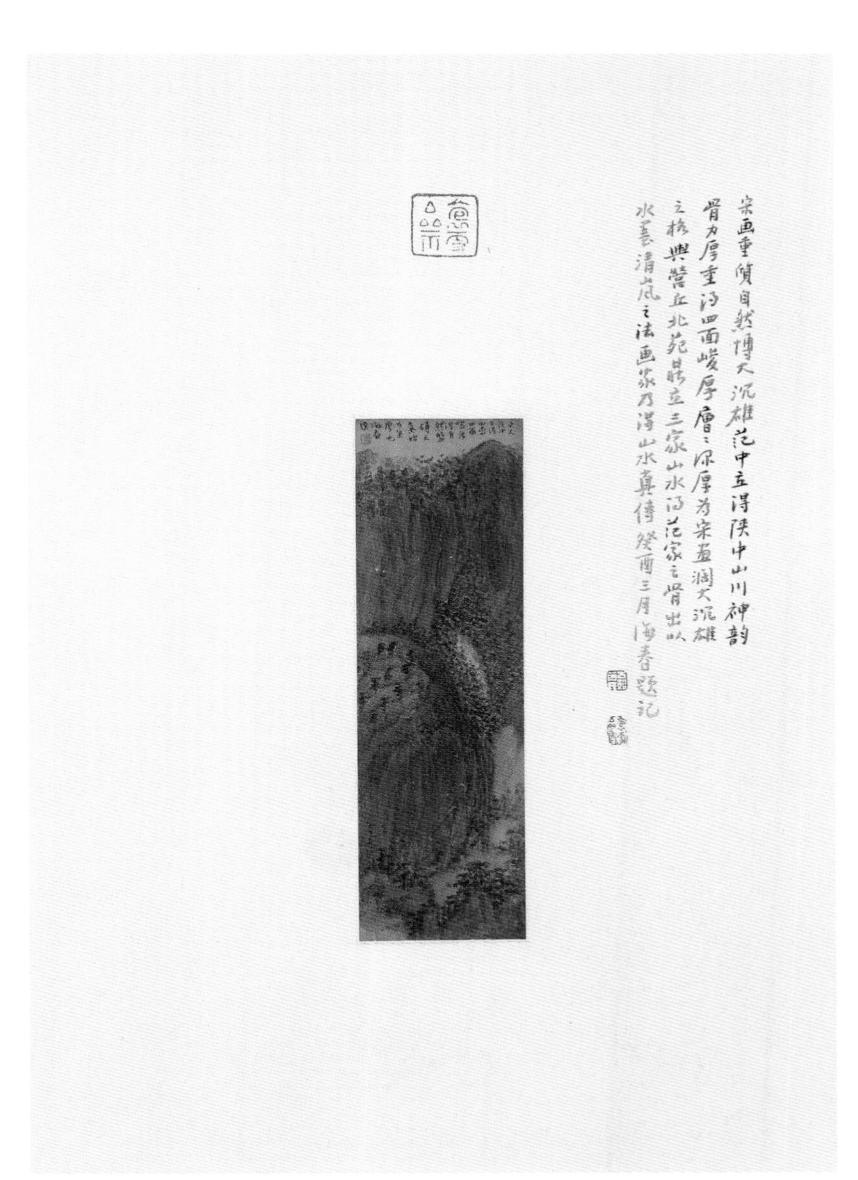

以小觀大冊
Mountain and River Scenery Series 6

1993
紙，水墨，冊頁
Album leaf, ink on paper.
23x7.1cm

以小觀大冊
Mountain and River Scenery Series 7

1993
紙，水墨，冊頁
Album leaf, ink on paper.
23x7.1cm

以小觀大冊

Mountain and River Scenery Series 8

1993

紙，水墨，冊頁

Album leaf, ink on paper.

23x7.1cm

以小觀大冊

Mountain and River Scenery Series 9

1993

紙，水墨，冊頁

Album leaf, ink on paper.

23x7.1cm

畫者能靜 靜則境深寬 靜以致遠 遠則杳冥幽漠 畫靜則
須人靜 自然與心境相映照 自然內美得以參悟 畫靜則
筆能靜 氣結太古積殷周冰雪以月上中天明鏡澄碧若華
艷流溢一時 處靜畫靜則人靜也 癸酉 桃花三月 雨海春題

山水逸格非草草而踈然非五日一石十日一水而為之逸致不在筆墨之多寡而在意趣分出徑庭山水本在趣上得其真宰倪雲林聊寫胸中逸氣然絕非逸筆草草觀其畫雖淡如秋影但層層皴擦筆致勁利淡而意密筆在厚腴故逸品不在筆墨而在趣雲林身後寂寞時人不識雲林遂開粗疏之時弊癸酉海春題記

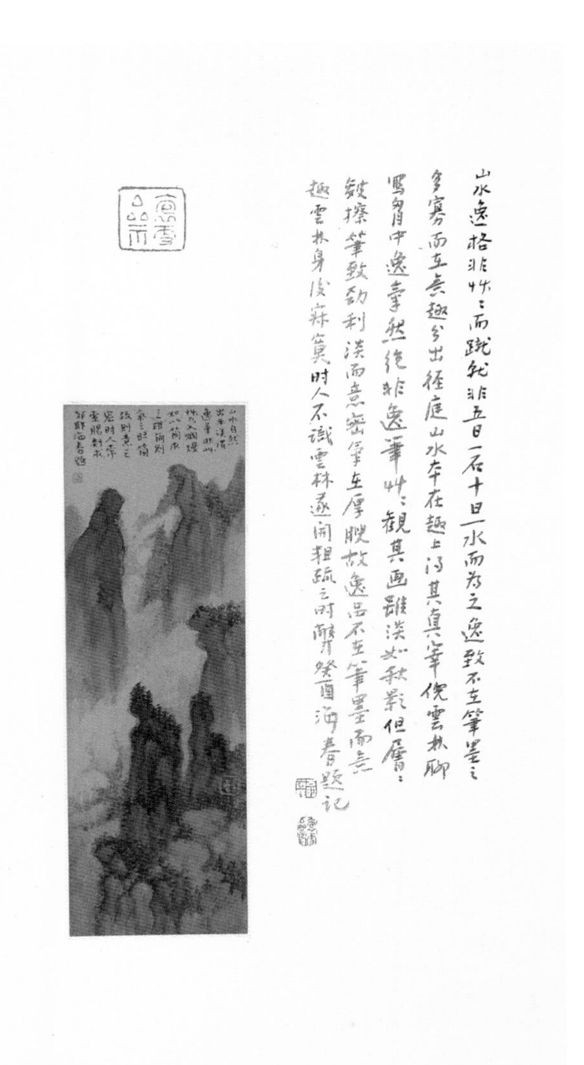

以小觀大冊

Mountain and River Scenery Series 10

1993

紙，設色，冊頁

Album leaf, ink and color on paper.

23x7.1cm

以小觀大冊

Essence of Mountain Series: Mountain and River Scenery Series 11

1993

紙，設色，冊頁

Album leaf, ink and color on paper.

23x7.1cm

雲壑松泉圖
Pine and Stream in Cloudy valley

1996
紙，淺設色，軸
Hanging scroll, ink and light color on paper.
393x141.3cm

谿山拾級圖

Climbing the Steps in Xishan

1996

紙，淺設色，軸

Hanging scroll, ink and light color on paper.

315x135.4cm

崔嵬當寒空
Cold Mountain

1997
紙，水墨，軸
Hanging scroll, ink on paper.
208x99cm

清光落煙樹
Misty Trees in Sunlight

1997
紙，水墨，軸
Hanging scroll, ink on paper.
208x99cm

疏雨山色外
Hills in Showers

1997
紙，水墨，軸
Hanging scroll, ink on paper.
208x99cm

三月草長時
Long Grass in March

1997
紙，水墨，軸
Hanging scroll, ink on paper.
180.5x103.1cm

陰陽割昏曉

Sun and Moon at Break of Dawn and Dusk

1997

紙，水墨，軸

Hanging scroll, ink on paper.

358x139.5cmx3

微霞抹青山
Green Mountains in Rosy Clouds

1998
紙，淺設色，軸
Hanging scroll, ink and light color on paper.
96x44.4cm

泉聲咽危石

Rocks Amid the Cacophony of Mountain Stream

1998

紙，淺設色，軸

Hanging scroll, ink and light color on paper.

89.9x39.9cm

空蒙上翠微
Hills Touched by Drizzle

1998
紙，水墨，軸
Hanging scroll, ink on paper.
59.9x46.6cm

雲起半明晦

Moon Enveloped by Clouds

1998

紙，淺設色，軸

Hanging scroll, ink and light color on paper.

81.7x40.2cm

漱石有清音

The Sound of Streams

1998

紙，淺設色，軸

Hanging scroll, ink and light color on paper.

82.4x39.7cm

野色呈秋意

Autumn View

1998

紙，淺設色，橫軸

Hanging scroll, ink and light color on paper.

44.2x95.7cm

庚辰海粟畫

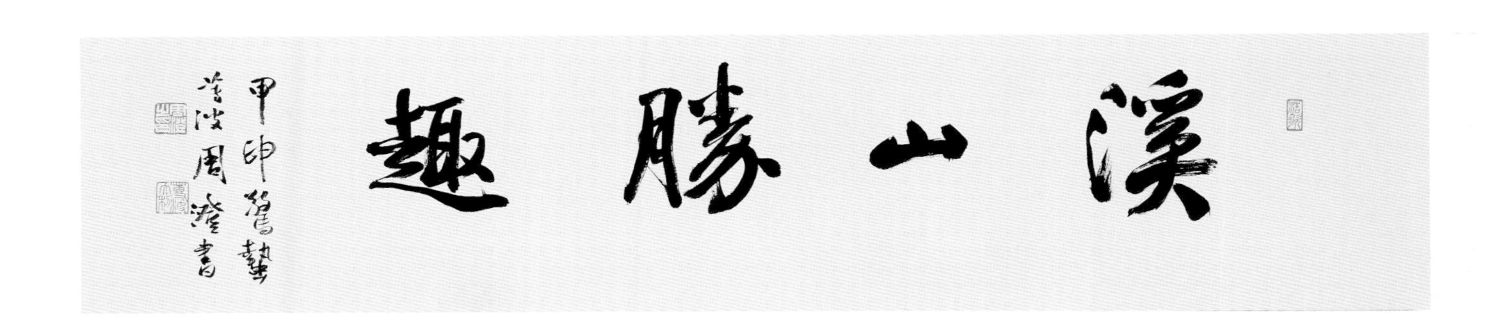

溪山勝趣

A Picturesque Mountains and Streams

1999

紙，淺設色，卷

Hand scroll, ink and light color on paper.

21.8x693.3cm

引首：21.8x102.4cm

溪山勝趣（局部）
A Picturesque Mountains and Streams

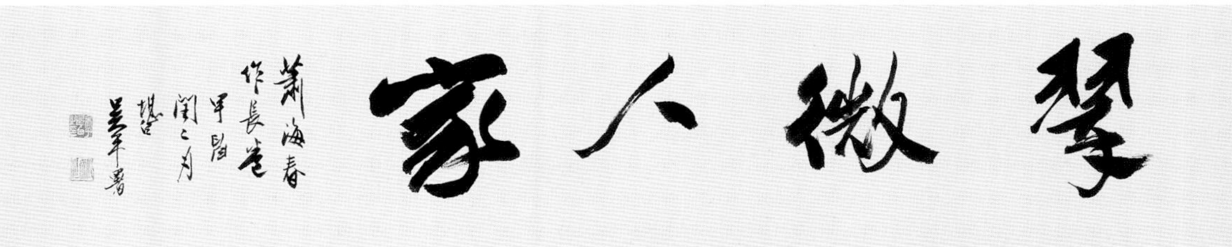

翠微人家
Villages among the Mountains

1999
紙，水墨，卷
Hand scroll, ink on paper.
22x691cm
引首：22x117cm

翠微人家（局部）
Villages among the Mountains

山水有清音

Melodies of the Hills and Valleys

1999

紙，淺設色，卷

Hand scroll, ink and light color on paper.

33.4x139cm

故山似畫屏

Picturesque Mountains

1999

紙，淺設色，卷

Hand scroll, ink and light color on paper.

33.4x139cm

遠色隱秋山
Distant Hills in Autumn

1999
紙，淺設色，卷
Hand scroll, ink and light color on paper.
33.4x139cm

山靜似太谷

Deserted Ancient Forest

1999

紙，淺設色，卷

Hand scroll, ink and light color on paper.

33.4x139cm

江流有遠聲

Murmurs of the Great River

1999

紙，水墨，卷

Hand scroll, ink on paper.

33.3x138.6cm

春半水爭流

Rivers in Mid-spring

1999

紙，淺設色，卷

Hand scroll, ink and light color on paper.

33.3x138.6cm

夏木蕭疏雲

Trees and Drifting Clouds in Summer

1999

紙，淺設色，卷

Hand scroll, ink and light color on paper.

33.3x138.6cm

百歲
惟傳
黃大
癡雲
山亂
石借
題詩
狂來
潑墨
同飲
酒誰
道游
仙不
畫師

2000～2003

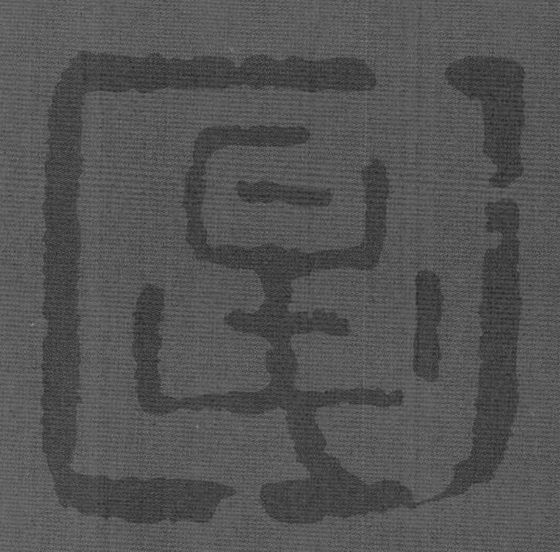

隱居結蓮社圖卷擬弘仁筆意

A Secluded House in the Manner of Hong Ren

2000

紙，淺設色，卷

Hand scroll, ink and light color on paper.

41.4x455.8cm

引首：41.4x96.3cm

蕭海春隱居結蓮社圖卷

文珠閣主人典藏 屬題

甲申閏二月 李蕭錕

栖巒圖

庚辰五月海山

千巖聳秀

甲申初春

翠崖棲幽

Secluded Cliff

2000

紙，淺設色，卷

Hand scroll, ink and light color on paper.

21.3x691.3cm

引首：21.3x103.2cm

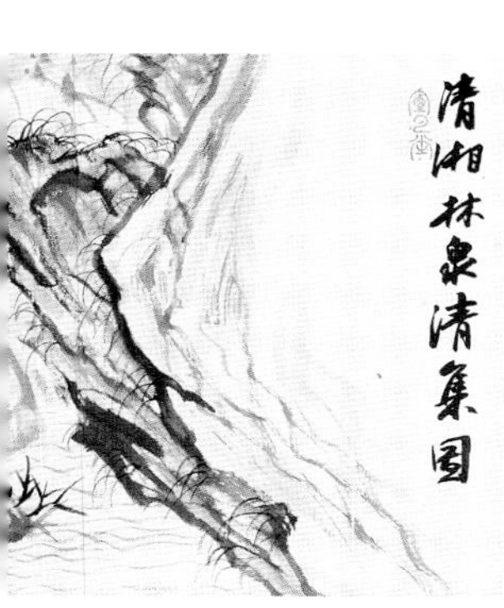

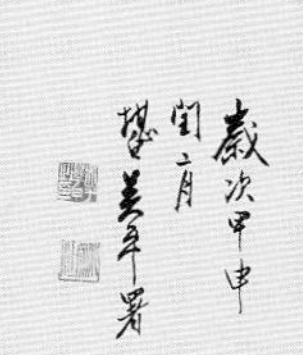

蕭海春仿清湘林泉清集圖

擬石濤林泉清集

A Replica of Shi Tao

2000

紙，水墨，卷

Hand scroll, ink and light color on paper.

29.5x302.6cm

引首：27.5x99.5cm

清湘林泉清集圖

溪山漁隱

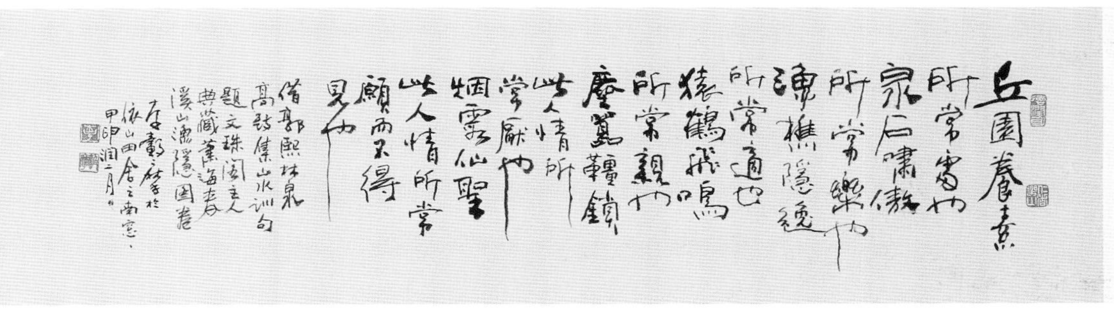

溪山漁隱

A Fisherman's Hut in the Mountain

2000

紙，淺設色，卷

Hand scroll, ink and light color on paper.

19x359cm

引首：19x89.7cm

煙雲變幻圖

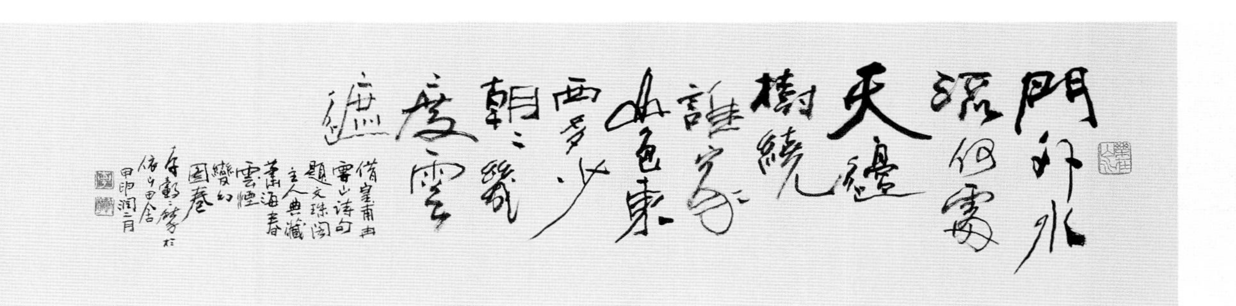

煙雲變幻

Changing Cloud Patterns

2000

紙，淺設色，卷

Hand scroll, ink and light color on paper.

18.5x678.2cm

引首：18.5x96cm

松頂自與峯巒黑
雲景何如水意閒
放下度節成心態
不妨生對日衡山
周澄書

松谷談清陰

Pine Valley in a Clear Night

2000
紙，水墨，軸
Hanging scroll, ink on paper.
142.2x120cm
詩塘：29.6x120cm

重岡細草覆陂陀
風引松花落澗阿
茅屋雨餘雲氣濕
開門不厭好山多
甲申暮春 蕚汝周澄書

雨餘濕翠嶂

Mountain after the Rain

2000

紙，淺設色，軸

Hanging scroll, ink and light color on paper.

120x141.6cm

詩塘：34.5x141.6cm

黃山寫意

Sketches of Huangshan

2000

紙，水墨，軸

Hanging scroll, ink on paper.

232x56cmx2

蕭蕭山水秋

Autumn Wind in Hills and Valleys

2000

紙，設色，橫軸

Hanging scroll, ink and color on paper.

140x182.3cm

陽崖開遠春數峯遠樹橫深棲典霧冥潔宅凭茅葺密山含嵐巖陰長松亘堤立欲中
棲隱地景与圖畫通翠微緣路明回環抱溪入迴出物表塵相携素心集高僧像佛
理煙霄淨墨汙前身巨然師落筆豈可及九衢塵污人丹青羨原隱

山冷雨催紅

A Welcome Rain in the Hills

2000

紙，設色，橫軸

Hanging scroll, ink and color on paper.

104x182.3cm

山堂昨夜起秋風
景物蕭條便不同
豈是天公嫌冷淡
故將林木染黃紅
元吳鎮題
次雲林韻
題耕雲東軒
讀易圖
甲申春日

曉霜丹葉

Morning Dew and Autumn Leaf

2001

紙，淺設色，軸

Hanging scroll, ink and light color on paper.

40x82cm

詩塘：19.7x82cm

四郭青山處處同客懷無計答秋風數家茅屋清溪上千樹蟬聲落日中

唐戴叔倫題友人山居

甲申春分尊汝周澄書於居山堂

太古人家

Village of Taikoo

2001

紙，淺設色，軸

Hanging scroll, ink and light color on paper.

40x82cm

詩塘：19.7x82cm

嘉谷籠煙

Valley and Mist

2001

紙，淺設色，軸

Hanging scroll, ink and light color on paper.

40x82cm

詩塘：19.7x82cm

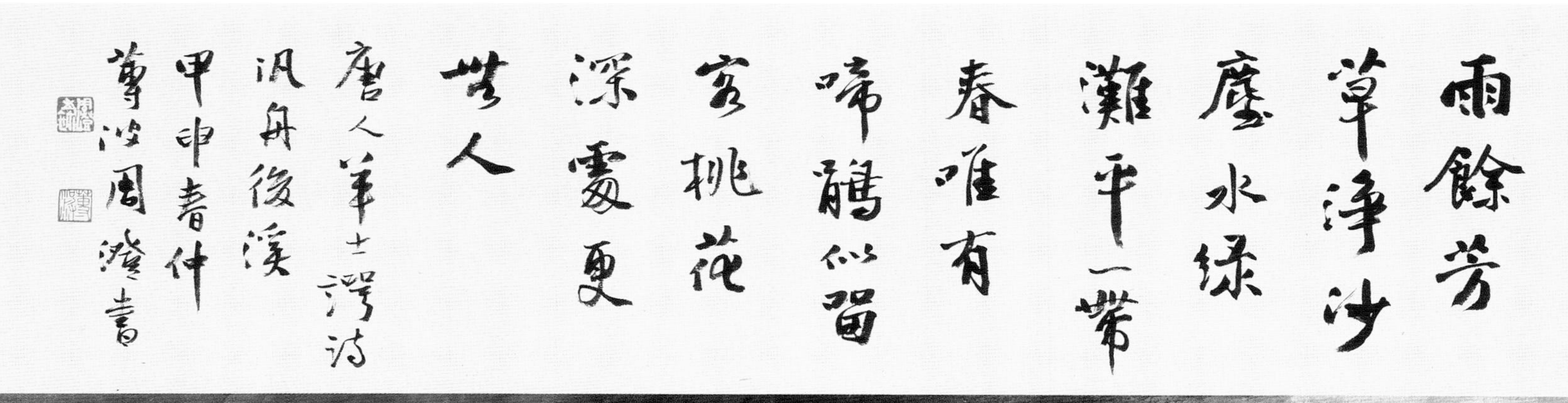

嵐霧鎖映

Reflections in Clouds and Fog

2001

紙，淺設色，軸

Hanging scroll, ink and light color on paper.

40x82cm

詩塘：19.7x82cm

林泉清集

Trees and Clear Rivers

2001

紙，淺設色，軸

Hanging scroll, ink and light color on paper.

67x67.5cm

詩塘：22x67.5cm

林泉清趣

甲申春日
蓉波周澄書

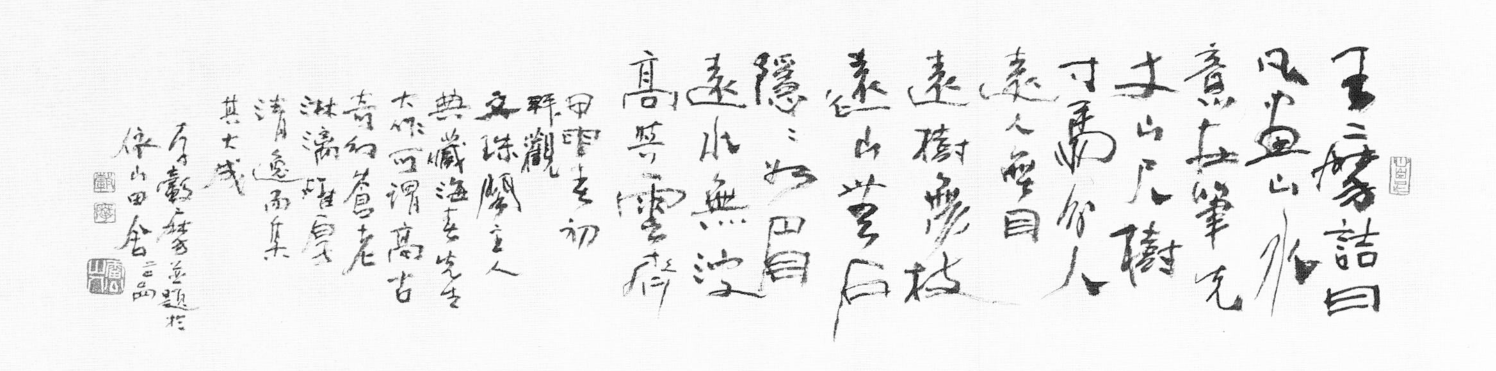

雨洗月痕新

Moonlit Night after Rain

2001

紙，水墨，軸

Hanging scroll, ink on paper.

67x67.5cm

詩塘：22x67.5cm

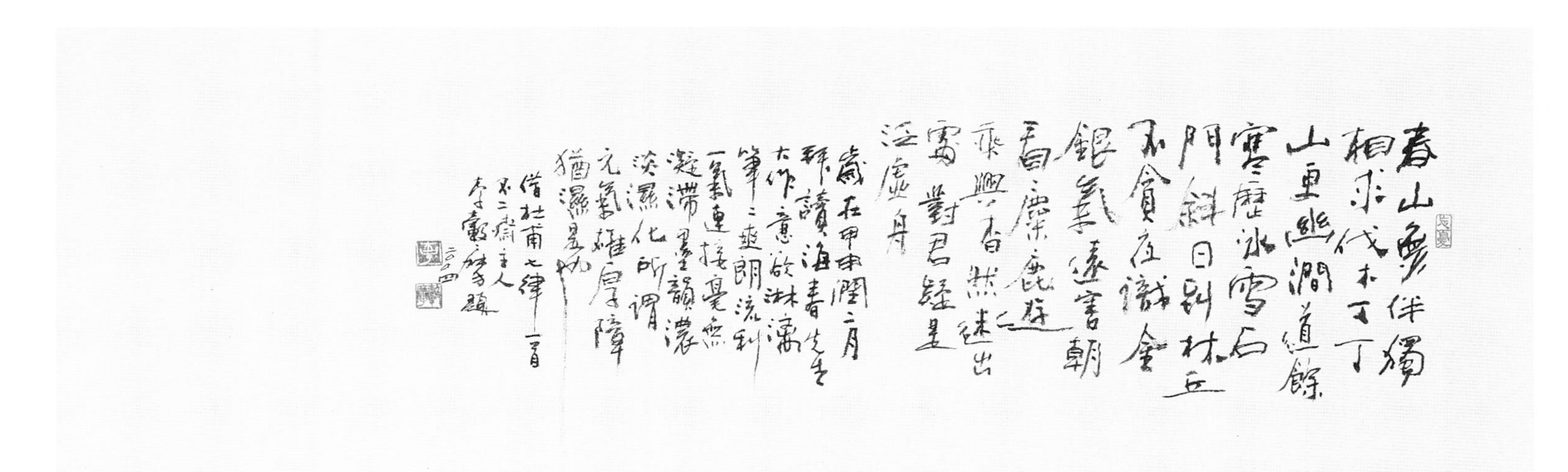

流光凝翠碧

Trees Cast in Sunlight

2001

紙，淺設色，軸

Hanging scroll, ink and light color on paper.

67x67.5cm

詩塘：22x67.5cm

紫氣東來

Blessings from the East

2001

紙，水墨，軸

Hanging scroll, ink on paper.

67x67.5cm

詩塘：22x67.5cm

秋雲歸壑

Cloud-shrouded Pointed Ridges in Autumn

2001

紙，淺設色，軸

Hanging scroll, ink and light color on paper.

67x67.5cm

詩塘：22x67.5cm

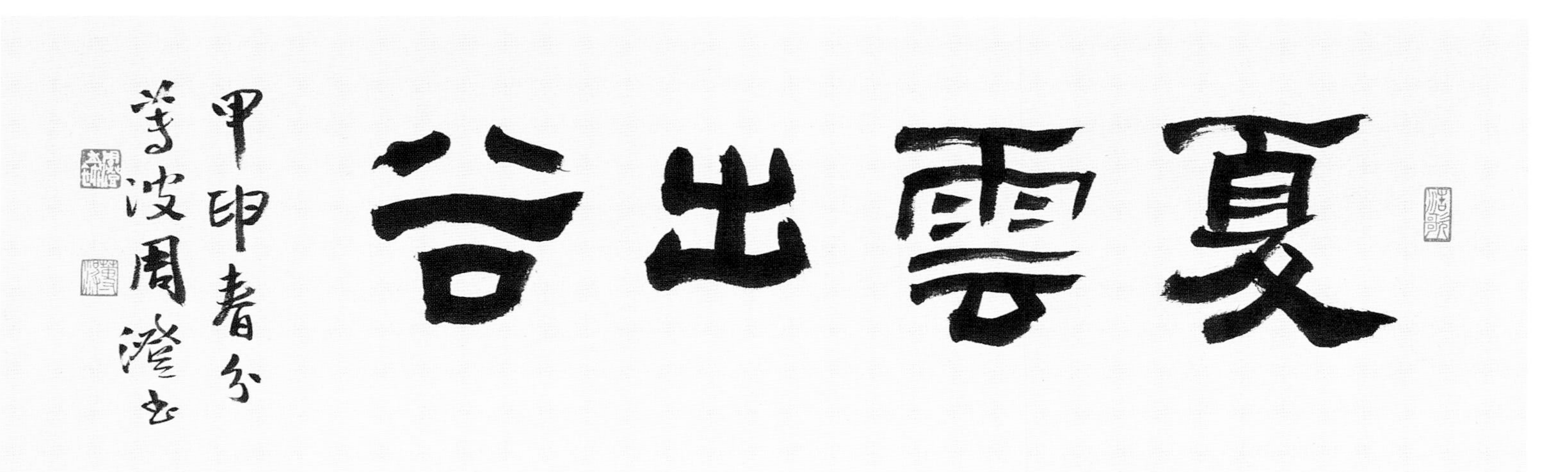

夏雲出谷

Cloudy Valley in Summer

2001

紙，淺設色，軸

Hanging scroll, ink and light color on paper.

67x67.5cm

詩塘：22x67.5cm

清潤雨餘天
Silvery Rain

2001
紙，淺設色，軸
Hanging scroll, ink and light color on paper.
60.8x47.5cm

野舍時雨潤

Secluded Hut after the Rain

2001

紙，淺設色，軸

Hanging scroll, ink and light color on paper.

60.8x47.5cm

山雜夏雲多
Summer Clouds

2001
紙，淺設色，軸
Hanging scroll, ink and light color on paper.
60.8x47.5cm

茂林延流光

Dense Forest Lost in Time

2001

紙，淺設色，軸

Hanging scroll, ink and light color on paper.

60.8x47.5cm

雲峰曉翠

蕭海春畫
文珠閣珍藏
甲申三月
蓴波周澄題

雲峰曉翠

Peak and Valley in Dawn

2001

紙，水墨，軸

Hanging scroll, ink on paper.

142.2x120cm

詩塘：29.6x120cm

巖巒鬱構澗路分松花一徑落紛紛何須著屐尋山去時有鐘聲出白雲

清王翬詩 甲申初春 菁沙周澄書

疏星淡月微

Pale Moon and Stars

2001

紙，淺設色，軸

Hanging scroll, ink and light color on paper.

120x141.6cm

詩塘：34.5x141.6cm

杳杳千峰失

A Thousand Peaks in the Distance

2001

紙，淺設色，軸

Hanging scroll, ink and light color on paper.

197.4x97cm

霧迷山月昏
Misty Hill in Twilight

2001
紙，淺設色，軸
Hanging scroll, ink and light color on paper.
197.4x97cm

雲浮青山瘦

The Hills and Parting Clouds

2001

紙，淺設色，軸

Hanging scroll, ink and light color on paper.

197.4x97cm

白霧魚飛氣黑雲牛馬形

雲擁山浮翠
Lively Forest on a Cloudy Day

2001
紙，淺設色，軸
Hanging scroll, ink and light color on paper.
180.2x190.2cm

夜色籠寒煙

Cold Mist Shrouding the Night

2001

紙，淺設色，軸

Hanging scroll, ink and light color on paper.

192.6x179.2cm

河聲入海遙

Songs in the Distant Sea

2001

紙，設色，橫幅

Hanging scroll, ink and color on paper.

123.4x247.3cm

入海口

具區林屋圖擬王蒙筆意
Hut in the Forest (A Copy of Wang Meng)

2002
紙，淺設色，軸
Hanging scroll, ink and color on paper.
178.6x96cm

霜寒半日畝 擬半千筆意

Frosty Field (A Copy of Banqian)

2002

紙，淺設色，軸

Hanging scroll, ink and light color on paper.

178.6x96cm

雲滿山頭樹滿谿
春風浩蕩綠初齊
若教世地容高隱
我不移家傍水西

周澄書

雲藏翠微

Cloud-covered Hills

2002

紙，淺設色，軸

Hanging scroll, ink and light color on paper.

142.2x120cm

詩塘：29.6x120cm

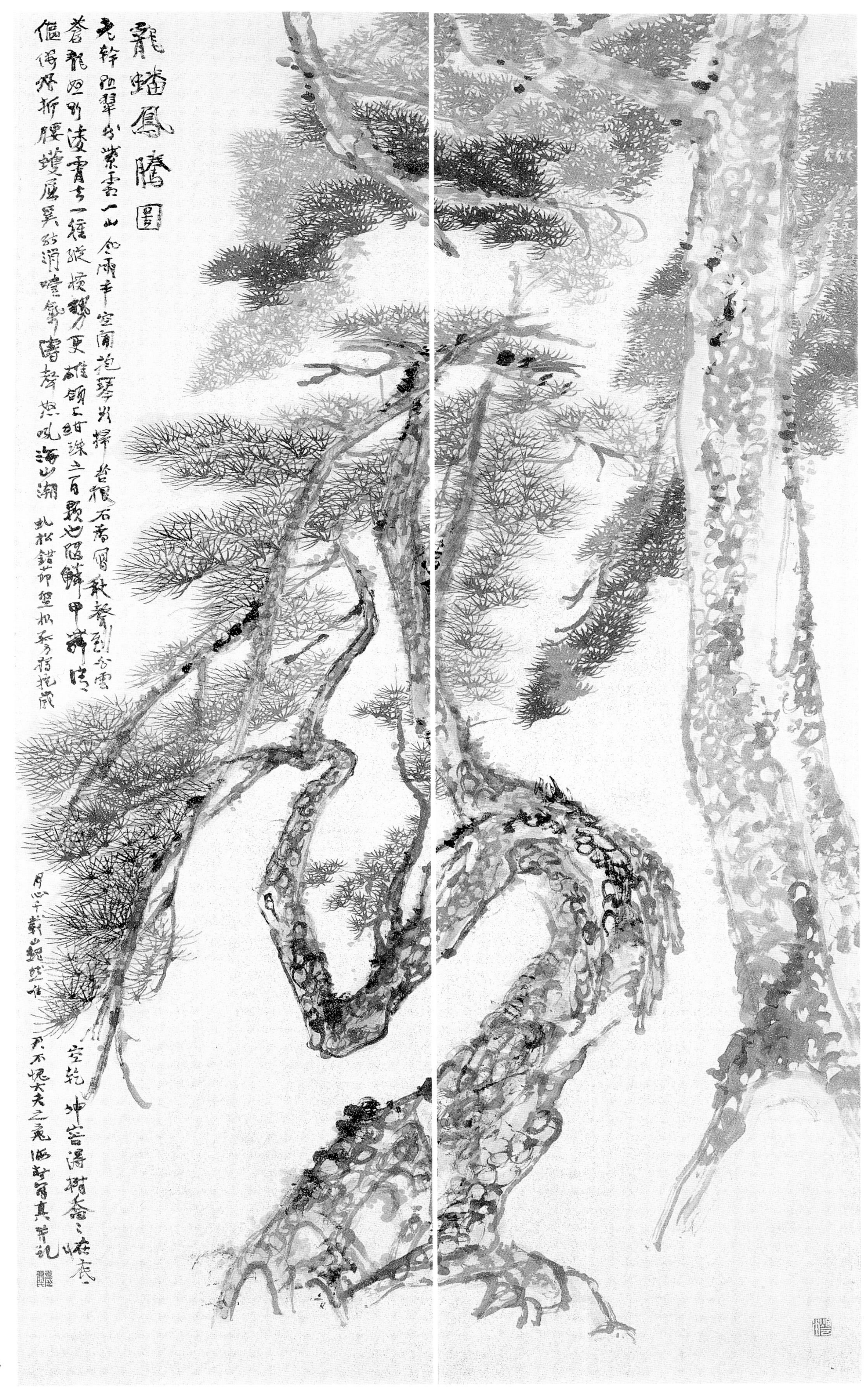

龍蟠鳳騰圖
Sleeping Dragon and
Soaring Phoenix

2002
紙，水墨，軸
Hanging scroll, ink on paper.
140x23.5cm

珊瑚碧珠圖

Pearl among Corals

2002

紙，設色，軸

Hanging scroll, ink and color on paper.

210x23.5cm

擬巨然筆意

In the Manner of Juran

2003

紙，淺設色，軸

Hanging scroll, ink and light color on paper.

245.2x92cm

2004

岩壑清音

Melodies of the Gorges

2004

紙，淺設色，冊頁

Album leaf, ink and light color on paper

34x34cm

春山煙靄

Mountain and Clouds in Spring

2004

紙，淺設色，冊頁

Album leaf, ink and light color on paper

34x34cm

岩鎖翠煙

Forest Mist among Cliffs

2004

紙，淺設色，冊頁

Album leaf, ink and light color on paper

34x34cm

閒雲無心

Drifting Clouds

2004

紙，淺設色，冊頁

Album leaf, ink and light color on paper

34x34cm

雨收黛青

Greeneries after the Rain

2004

紙，淺設色，冊頁

Album leaf, ink and light color on paper

34x34cm

白雲紅樹

Red Trees and White Clouds

2004

紙，淺設色，冊頁

Album leaf, ink and light color on paper

34x34cm

斷霞散彩

Brilliance of Dusk Clouds

2004

紙，淺設色，冊頁

Album leaf, ink and light color on paper

34x34cm

嘉木繁陰

A Dense Forest

2004

紙，淺設色，冊頁

Album leaf, ink and light color on paper

34x34cm

清露滴幽

Secluded Valley Covered in Dew

2004

紙，淺設色，冊頁

Album leaf, ink and light color on paper

34x34cm

山靜太谷

Ancient Valley in Quiet Hill

2004

紙，淺設色，冊頁

Album leaf, ink and light color on paper

34x34cm

嘉谷籠煙

Valley and Mist

2004

紙，淺設色，冊頁

Album leaf, ink and light color on paper

34x34cm

2004

紙，淺設色，冊頁

Album leaf, ink and light color on paper

34x34cm

萬樹畫秋聲

Ten Thousand Trees in Autumn

2004

紙，淺設色，軸

Hanging scroll, ink and light color on paper.

97x179.4cm

清秋雨新霽

Fresh From the Autumn Rain

2004

紙，淺設色，軸

Hanging scroll, ink and light color on paper.

179.4x97cm

泉泠溪頭樹
Silent Stream and the Tree

2004
紙，淺設色，軸
Hanging scroll, ink and light color on paper.
197.4x97cm

雲開對月明

Moon among Parting Clouds

2004

紙，淺設色，軸

Hanging scroll, ink and light color on paper.

197.4x97cm

雲開見山高
High Mountain amid Parting Clouds

2004
紙，淺設色，軸
Hanging scroll, ink and light color on paper.
197.4x97cm

千嶂收暮雲
Evening Clouds Hidden Behind Mountains

2004
紙，淺設色，軸
Hanging scroll, ink and light color on paper,
197.4x97cm

南山白雲閑

A Leisurely Nanshan

2004

紙，淺設色，軸

Hanging scroll, ink and light color on paper.

197.4x97cm

雲鎖兩三峰

Twin Peaks Shrouded in Clouds

2004

紙，淺設色，軸

Hanging scroll, ink and light color on paper.

197.4x97cm

雲淨山浮翠
Forested Hill on a Clear Day

2004
紙，淺設色，冊頁
Album leaf, ink and light color on paper
48x44.5cm

百丈裂素崖
High Cliff

2004
紙，淺設色，冊頁
Album leaf, ink and light color on paper
48x44.5cm

素月籠煙谷

Pale Moon Overlooking Misty Valley

2004

紙，淺設色，冊頁

Album leaf, ink and light color on paper

48x44.5cm

露白月微明

Half-seen Moon at Dawn

2004

紙，淺設色，冊頁

Album leaf, ink and light color on paper

48x44.5cm

月出驚山鳥

Pheasants in Rising Moon

2004

紙，淺設色，冊頁

Album leaf, ink and light color on paper

48x44.5cm

春雲出岫秀

Young Mountain Emerging from the Clouds

2004

紙，淺設色，冊頁

Album leaf, ink and light color on paper

48x44.5cm

夕臥白雲閑

Evening and Lazy Clouds

2004

紙，淺設色，冊頁

Album leaf, ink and light color on paper

48x44.5cm

日長如小年

A Long Day

2004

紙，淺設色，冊頁

Album leaf, ink and light color on paper

48x44.5cm

日落秋色遠

Dusk in Autumn

2004

紙，淺設色，冊頁

Album leaf, ink and light color on paper

48x44.5cm

翠嶺秋天外

Lush Mountains in Autumn

2004

紙，淺設色，冊頁

Album leaf, ink and light color on paper

48x44.5cm

春物有餘妍

Lingering Spring Beauty

2004

紙，淺設色，冊頁

Album leaf, ink and light color on paper

48x44.5cm

長夜歇芳菲

A Long Night

2004

紙，淺設色，冊頁

Album leaf, ink and light color on paper

48x44.5cm

秋雲靜山林

Peaceful Forest in Autumn

2004

紙，淺設色，軸

Hanging scroll, ink and light color on paper.

97x179.4cm

遙山翠色同

Lush Distant Hills

2004

紙，淺設色，軸

Hanging scroll, ink and light color on paper.

97x179.4cm

雲靜山浮翠

Lively Forested Hill on a Still Day

2004

紙，淺設色，軸

Hanging scroll, ink and light color on paper.

97x179.4cm

空濛上翠微

Hills Touched by Drizzle

2004

紙，淺設色，軸

Hanging scroll, ink and light color on paper.

197.4x97cm

嶺高松更疏
A Few Pines Among Cliffs

2004
紙，淺設色，軸
Hanging scroll, ink and light color on paper.
197.4x97cm

長虹落青冥
The Yangtze Joins the Great Sea

2004
紙，淺設色，軸
Hanging scroll, ink and light color on paper.
197.4x97cm

雲斷半銜青

Broken Clouds

2004

紙，淺設色，軸

Hanging scroll, ink and light color on paper.

179.4x97cm

群嶂摩天垠

At Sky's Edge

2004

紙，淺設色，軸

Hanging scroll, ink and light color on paper.

97x179.4cm

四景宜畫屏

Four Seasons

2004

紙，設色，卷

Hand scroll, ink and light color on paper.

55x574cm

四景宜畫屏

蒼然萬山色

Imposing Forested Hills

2004

紙，淺設色，軸

Hanging scroll, ink and light color on paper.

97x179.4cm

丹崖一徑通

Narrow Path in Red Cliff

2004

紙，淺設色，軸

Hanging scroll, ink and light color on paper.

179.4x97cm

突兀上龍背

To Touch the Dragon

2004

紙，淺設色，軸

Hanging scroll, ink and light color on paper.

179.4x97cm

瑞氣淩青空
Blessings in Blue Sky

2004
紙，淺設色，軸
Hanging scroll,
ink and light color on paper.
179.4x97cm

微雨洗山骨

Hills Drenched in Shower

2004

紙，淺設色，軸

Hanging scroll, ink and light color on paper.

137.8x68.8cm

摩詰詩意

Insight into Poetic Beauty

2004

紙，淺設色，橫軸

Hanging scroll, ink and light color on paper.

51.2x260cm

明月松間照清泉石上流摩詰詩意

嵯峨起百重

Immense Mountain Range

2004

紙，淺設色，軸

Hanging scroll, ink and light color on paper.

138x137.3cm

峨峨上翠芳

Lush High Mountains

2004

紙，淺設色，軸

Hanging scroll, ink and light color on paper.

137x137.6cm

雨歇晚霞明

Evening Clouds after Rain

2004

紙，淺設色，軸

Hanging scroll, ink and light color on paper.

137.8x68.8cm

千山翠欲浮

Lively Forested Mountains

2004

紙，淺設色，軸

Hanging scroll, ink and light color on paper.

137.8x68.8cm

流雲散翠崖

Cliff Covered by Clouds

2004

紙，淺設色，軸

Hanging scroll, ink and light color on paper.

137.8x68.8cm

摩詰詩意

Insight into Poetic Beauty

2004

紙，淺設色，軸

Hanging scroll, ink and light color on paper.

137.8x68.8cm

林泉真意冊　素月流天

Essence of Country Sceneries Series: Pale Moon 1

2004

紙，淺設色，斗方

Album leaf mounted as panel, ink and color on paper

24x27cm

林泉真意冊　霜倒池蓮

Essence of Country Sceneries Series: Lotus Pond in Autumn 2

2004

紙，淺設色，斗方

Album leaf mounted as panel, ink and color on paper

24x27cm

林泉真意冊　清夏潺湲

Essence of Country Sceneries Series: Running Stream in Summer 3

2004

紙，淺設色，斗方

Album leaf mounted as panel, ink and color on paper

24x27cm

林泉真意冊　秋林遠黛

Essence of Country Sceneries Series: Distant Forest in Late Autumn 4

2004

紙，淺設色，斗方

Album leaf mounted as panel, ink and color on paper

24x27cm

山靜似太古日長如小年餘花猶可醉好鳥不妨眠
宋人詩意

林泉真意冊　晚晴秋老

Essence of Country Sceneries Series: Late Autumn Evening 5

2004

紙，淺設色，斗方

Album leaf mounted as panel, ink and color on paper

24x27cm

林泉真意冊　雨餘山幽

Essence of Country Sceneries Series: Secluded Hills after the Rain 6

2004

紙，淺設色，斗方

Album leaf mounted as panel, ink and color on paper

24x27cm

林泉真意冊　林泉高致

Essence of Country Sceneries Series:

Of Retirement in the Countryside 7

2004

紙，淺設色，斗方

Album leaf mounted as panel, ink and color on paper

24x27cm

林泉真意冊　春靜山空

Essence of Country Sceneries Series:

Deserted Hills in a Still Spring Day 8

2004

紙，淺設色，斗方

Album leaf mounted as panel, ink and color on paper

24x27cm

林泉真意冊　綠野秀踪

Essence of Country Sceneries Series: Greenfields 9

2004

紙，淺設色，斗方

Album leaf mounted as panel, ink and color on paper

24x27cm

林泉真意冊　聳翠深樹

Essence of Country Sceneries Series:

Looming Trees and Deep Forest 10

2004

紙，淺設色，斗方

Album leaf mounted as panel, ink and color on paper

24x27cm

留住彩霧香雲冊

Of Rosy Glow and Fragrant Clouds Series 1

2004

紙，設色，斗方

Album leaf mounted as panel, ink and color on paper

diam. 21cm

留住彩霧香雲冊

Of Rosy Glow and Fragrant Clouds Series 2

2004

紙，設色，斗方

Album leaf mounted as panel, ink and color on paper

diam. 21cm

留住彩霧香雲冊

Of Rosy Glow and Fragrant Clouds Series 3

2004

紙，設色，斗方

Album leaf mounted as panel, ink and color on paper

diam. 21cm

留住彩霧香雲冊

Of Rosy Glow and Fragrant Clouds Series 4

2004

紙，設色，斗方

Album leaf mounted as panel, ink and color on paper

diam. 21cm

六月清涼綠樹陰小亭高卧滌煩襟羲皇向上
何人到永日時〻弄素琴 唐人詩意
海岳

留住彩霧香雲冊
Of Rosy Glow and Fragrant Clouds Series 5

2004
紙，設色，斗方
Album leaf mounted as panel, ink and color on paper
diam. 21cm

留住彩霧香雲冊
Of Rosy Glow and Fragrant Clouds Series 6

2004
紙，設色，斗方
Album leaf mounted as panel, ink and color on paper
diam. 21cm

留住彩霧香雲冊
Of Rosy Glow and Fragrant Clouds Series 7

2004
紙，設色，斗方
Album leaf mounted as panel, ink and color on paper
diam. 21cm

留住彩霧香雲冊
Of Rosy Glow and Fragrant Clouds Series 8

2004
紙，設色，斗方
Album leaf mounted as panel, ink and color on paper
diam. 21cm

山人愛山如李白幽棲遠在碧雲深松杉繞屋清霄響雷雨懸巖白晝陰 元人詩意 海峯

留住彩霧香雲冊
Of Rosy Glow and Fragrant Clouds Series 9

2004
紙，設色，斗方
Album leaf mounted as panel, ink and color on paper
diam. 21cm

留住彩霧香雲冊
Of Rosy Glow and Fragrant Clouds Series 10

2004
紙，設色，斗方
Album leaf mounted as panel, ink and color on paper
diam. 21cm

山中真意冊　春深紅十里
Essence of Mountain Series: Late Spring 1

2004
紙，設色，斗方
Album leaf mounted as panel, ink and color on paper
diam. 21cm

山中真意冊　遠芳侵古道
Essence of Mountain Series: Ancient Pathway 2

2004
紙，設色，斗方
Album leaf mounted as panel, ink and color on paper
diam. 21cm

山中真意冊　山中有真意
The Essence of Mountains 3

2004
紙，設色，斗方
Album leaf mounted as panel, ink and color on paper
diam. 21cm

山中真意冊　野雲共秋白
Essence of Mountain Series: Clouds are Pale as Autumn 4

2004
紙，設色，斗方
Album leaf mounted as panel, ink and color on paper
diam. 21cm

山中真意冊　山冷雨催紅
Essence of Mountain Series: The Relief of Rain 5

2004
紙，設色，斗方
Album leaf mounted as panel, ink and color on paper
diam. 21cm

山中真意冊　夜靜春山空
Essence of Mountain Series: Deserted Hills in a Quiet Spring Night 6

2004
紙，設色，斗方
Album leaf mounted as panel, ink and color on paper
diam. 21cm

山中真意冊　曉夕重輕煙
Essence of Mountain Series: Misty Morning 7

2004
紙，設色，斗方
Album leaf mounted as panel, ink and color on paper
diam. 21cm

山中真意冊　墟外日遲遲
Essence of Mountain Series: Deserted House in Late Evening 8

2004
紙，設色，斗方
Album leaf mounted as panel, ink and color on paper
diam. 21cm

勢似孤峰一片成坐來疑有白雲生主人莫怪殷勤看遠客長懷舊隱情

青溪宜曉日曲盡千丈臨天開蒼石屏影落西村外

寫古人詩意

海舟并題

山中真意冊
Essence of Mountain Series: Essence of Mountain Series 9

2004
紙，設色，斗方
Album leaf mounted as panel, ink and color on paper
diam. 21cm

山中真意冊　江樹晚逾青
Essence of Mountain Series: Trees Along the Riverbank 10

2004
紙，設色，斗方
Album leaf mounted as panel, ink and color on paper
diam. 21cm

空山流水圖
Empty Mountains and Streams

2004
紙，淺設色，卷
Hand scroll, ink and light color on paper.
51x356.5cm

空山流水圖

山水冊 擬石濤筆意
Album Leaves of Mountains and Streams in the Manner of Shitao

2004
紙，淺設色，冊頁
Album leaf, ink and light color on paper.
34x34cm

清湘老人
濟

畫到無
聲何敢
題句
清湘苦瓜
老人濟

荒邨建子月獨
樹老夫家
瞎眼尊者

言携青玉杖千折上雲霄
老濤

牛首土山多
平臺々上々土人
皆種菜麦遠
望平林始信大
癡黃鶴山樵
蒼々點法
石濤

閑水閑
山必自
有意

翁源多
畫意
到此得
其心自能
潭上有
此苦瓜老
人濟

遙〻
望白
雲懷
古一
何深
濟

是濃非法
即成我法十
二冊寄上
禹老道兄正
苦瓜和尚濟

蓮林入不覺
獨樹衆乃奇
濟

濟

荒亭岑寂荒山裏老樹無花傍水磯飯後
尋幽偶到此十分寒苦慘斜暉濟

山色蒼〻
樹色秋
黃雲欲
碎背飄
流
瞎尊者

雨後泉聲煙樹
傳人家淺水隔山
田東西出入門無
路多是谿邊有
小船 石濤

古人徑無人流水折空
谷幽鳥識春心
響音入千山腹
苦瓜老人濟

清湘小乘
客濟

湖雁雙雙起人來
故北征枝下濟

石濤濟

去國三巴遠登樓萬春傷心
江上客不是故鄉人
濟

湖上秋山木葉飛
石粼〻水淺任魚
肥閒將小艇對住日
落西林載酒歸
小乘客石濤
濟

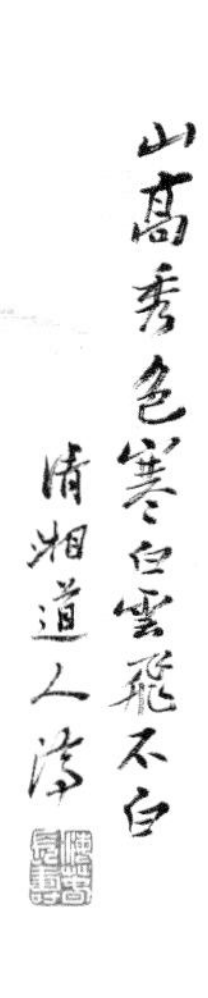
山高秀色寒白雲飛不白
清湘道人濟

去國三巴遠登樓萬春傷心
江上客不是故鄉人 濟

蕭海春生平年表

一九四四年　蕭海春生於上海，祖籍江西豐城，別署抱雪齋、煙雲堂。中國工藝美術大師，中國美術家協會上海分會會員，上海中國畫院兼職畫師，上海市突出貢獻專家協會會員。

一九六一年　蕭海春考入上海工藝美術學校，學習傳統繪畫與雕刻，曾受畫家王康樂、顧飛的指導，對於黃賓虹的繪畫藝術獨有興趣。

一九六四年　畢業於上滿工藝美術學校，入上海玉石雕刻廠，從事專業設計，潛心中國畫創作。

一九六五年　獲上海《青年報》舉辦的書畫創作大賽一等獎。國畫新作發表於《文匯報》、《青年報》等刊物。上海中國畫院王其元先生撰文推介。被《文匯報》、《青年報》聘爲美術通訊員。

一九六七年　赴雁蕩山寫生。

一九六八年　赴井岡山、長沙、西安、銅川、延安，後折入巴蜀，順江遊三峽。

一九七八年　入貴洲、雲南高原。獨喜大、小涼山之景。

一九八〇年　在上海人民公園舉辦《八人畫展》。

一九八二年　遊富春江，經紹興謁大禹陵、蘭亭。

一九八三年　二上雁蕩山。

在雲岡石窟 1983年

一九八四年　人物畫李白詩意《落日故人情》獲上海書畫出版社舉辦的全國“以詩征畫”大賽一等獎。《書與畫》雜誌作專題介紹。

柯文輝先生撰《拾級而上》一文評述。

赴廬山。

一九八五年　作西北之行。秦陵、霍去病墓、乾陵等，考察石刻藝術。

應中國畫研究院之請作《清清小河水》、《山居圖》，並爲該院收藏。

一九八六年　《中國畫》雜誌作專題介紹，柯文輝先生撰文評述。

再赴西北麥積山考察石刻藝術，經蘭洲，遊炳靈寺，西上張掖、武威、酒泉，至敦煌。穿祁連山，經峨堡大草原進入西寧，謁塔爾寺。旋又赴廬山。

一九八七年　再赴西寧，登華山，北上大同考察雲岡石窟，經太原，拜謁晉祠及平遙雙林寺，後折入洛陽，考察龍門石窟。

人物畫《八大山人》收入《上海美術年鑒》。連環畫《八大山人》由上海人民美術出版社出版發行。

《江蘇畫刊》專題介紹，王邦雄撰文評述。

一九八八年　山水畫《西行山水》參加上海青年國畫聯展。

程十髮先生在畫展 蕭海春·了廬畫展 1988年

作品參加上海美術館赴法國、意大利、比利時巡迴展。

山水畫《空穀》入選北京國際水墨畫展。

《美術叢刊》發表自撰文《尋找樂土》並發表其西行之作。

《朵雲》雜誌專題介紹。

赴黃山寫生。

獲“中國工藝美術大師”稱號。

與師傅們在一起 1990年

一九八九年　《朵雲》發表人物、山水作品。

作品參加上海朵雲軒的《江南山水畫展》。

應上海中國畫院之邀舉辦聯展。（蕭海春——了廬畫展）

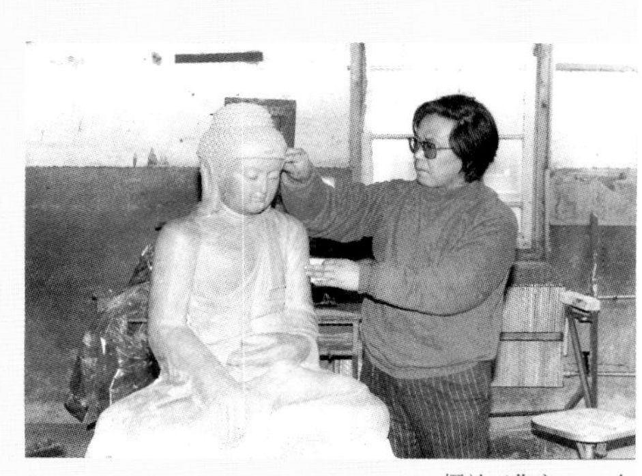

攝於工作室 1990年

一九九〇年　香港《藝術家》專題發表山水畫，莊藝嶺先生撰文評述。

香港《中國文物世界》專題介紹其山水畫，楊念月先生撰文評述。

大業公司出版《蕭海春畫展》。

選為《人才》雜誌封面人物。

一九九一年　與張仃、龍瑞、陳向迅、陳平、趙衛、盧禹舜等參加香港“三石軒”舉辦的山水畫聯展。

參加上海美術館主辦的蕭海春、陳心懋、朱敏、王天德四人聯展。

《上海畫報》人物專欄專題介紹，了廬先生撰文評述。作品收入《上海美術年鑒》。

接受上海《新民晚報》人物專題專欄介紹。

參加中國畫研究院主辦的“首屆中國山水畫聯展”。

一九九三年　參加上海美術館等主辦的《上海－臺北水墨畫聯展》。

入選中國藝術研究院主編的《中國畫大陸百人傳》。

作品入選《海上名家畫集》（上海人民美術出版社）。

作為海上山水畫代表在《畫廊》雜誌專題介紹，自撰《艱難歷程》一文談山水畫創作。

作品《早春氣息》獲“第二屆全國山水畫展”優秀獎和收藏獎。

一九九四年　在臺北敦煌藝術中心舉辦《再造河山無限意——蕭海春畫展》。

新加坡“莊藝術”舉行“蕭海春畫展”。

一九九五年　漢雅軒在香港藝術中心舉辦《蕭海春畫展》，徐展堂為展覽揭幕。

參加朵雲軒在上海美術館舉辦的《海上十五家畫展》，展出六屏條“月色荷塘”（60×240cm×6）。

江蘇畫刊95.2專題介紹山水作品。

參加上海美術館赴日本大阪現代中國畫展。

秋，有雁蕩、富春之遊。

一九九六年　參加中國畫院舉辦的新春畫展。

創作《紅蜻蜓》十屏花鳥（60×240cm×10）。

創作《百子圖》六屏花卉（60×240cm×6）。

參加上海美術館赴法蘭西現代中國畫展。

參加上海美術館赴德國現代中國畫展。

山水《井岡山》（95×178cm）、《朱砂雄關眞如鐵》（95×178cm）參加由中國美術家協會和中國畫研究院舉辦的《情系井岡——著名中國山水畫家創作展》。

上海電視臺《詩與畫》專欄作專題採訪。

應邀赴馬來西亞、新加坡遊覽。由馬來西亞敦煌藝術公司主辦的《蕭海春畫展》在吉隆坡帝苑酒店隆重舉行，馬來西亞郵電通訊部副部長，中國駐馬大使出席開幕酒會。應馬來西亞廣播電臺邀請作專題採訪。

參加朵雲軒、聯征古玩號舉辦的《聯征雲集——現代中國水墨畫展》，作品《招財樹》被選作畫展海報刊行。

一九九七年　赴新加坡參加由好望角畫廊舉辦的《傳統與創新——蕭海春作品精選展》。

在陰陽割昏曉巨作前 1997年

參加上海美術館赴俄羅斯現代中國畫展。

參加《慶祝中華人民共和國恢復對香港行使主權——中國藝術大展》。

參加《97'上海藝術博覽會》。

《龍脈》（100×210cm）、《摩詰詩意》（100×210cm）參加上海中國畫院建院三十五週年畫展。

出版《再造河山——蕭海春山水畫》掛曆。

《二十世紀中國水墨畫大系——蕭海春》由香港大業公司出版，邵大箴、朱乃正、盧輔聖、徐建融撰文。

一九九八年　創作《陰陽隔昏曉》（420×356cm），入選1998年古根漢舉辦的《五千年文明畫展－現代部分》。

作品《有幽可居》參加“98'中國國際美術年——當代中國山水畫_油畫風景展”。

參加“上海百家精品展”展出《紅蜻蜓》。

參加首屆“上海中國畫98'雙年展”。

與好友攝於黃山道中 2001年

與好友在畫展 2001年

揮酒與有酣 2002年

年年有餘 與好友在富陽華寶齋 2004

	赴黃山寫生。
	赴法國、盧森堡、荷蘭、比利時、德國、奧地利、意大利、瑞士等國考察。
一九九九年	應古吳軒編輯《當代水墨畫藝術新主張》系列叢書，入編“水墨山水。
	赴黃山寫生。
二〇〇〇年	參加李小山策劃“新中國畫大展”。
	入選《中國當代美術（中國畫）》畫冊。
	被編入《當代美術圖鑒》山水卷（湖北）。
	參加北京油畫協會在芬蘭舉辦的“當代油畫_中國畫展”。
二〇〇一年	參加中國美術協會舉辦的“百年中國畫展”。
	參加首屆全國畫院雙年展。
	參加歷屆上海中國畫院年展。
	入選“2001' 上海美術大展”。
	帶學生赴黃山寫生。
二〇〇二年	參加“中日書法藝術交流展”。
	上海《書與畫》名家聚焦專題介紹。（吳霖田採訪拍攝，自撰藝術劄記）
	春節，與家人雨中登黃山。
二〇〇三年	上海《書與畫》傳移摹寫專欄，連載“名家臨石濤”講評。
	劉海粟美術館“蕭海春水墨畫工作室”成立。
	參加全國畫院雙年展。
	參加上海中國畫院年展。
	被聘爲上海青年美術大展評委委員。
	帶學生登黃山寫生。
二〇〇四年	八月在國立歷史博物館舉行“名家水墨：黃秋園．蕭海春作品聯展”。
	上海書畫出版社出版《蕭海春名家臨石濤、龔賢》專集。

A Brief Profile of Xiao Haichun

1944 Born in Shanghai to a family from Feng Cheng, Chiangxi Province. Was also known as "Bao Xue Zhai" and "Yen Yun Tang". Master of the Chinese arts and craftsmanship. Member of the Shanghai branch of the Association of Chinese Artists. Part-time master painter of Shanghai Academy of Chinese Paintings (上海中國畫院). Member of the Association of Experts with Outstanding Contributions of Shanghai.

1961 Passed the entrance exam and was admitted to the School of Fine Arts and Art Design of Shanghai (上海工藝美術學校), majoring in traditional paintings and sculpture. Was taught by famous painters such as Wang Kang-Le and Gu Fei. Was particularly inspired by the art of Huang Bin-Hong's paintings.

1964 Graduated from the School of Fine Arts and Art Design of Shanghai. Was employed by Shanghai Gems Sculpture Factory (上海玉石雕刻廠) as a professional designer. Focused on the creation of Chinese paintings at the same time.

1965 Won the first-class award of the first paintings and calligraphy contest organized by Shanghai the "Youth Daily". New work of Chinese paintings were published on newspapers such as "Wen Hui Daily" and the "Youth Daily". Was recommended by Mr. Wang Qiyuan of the Shanghai Academy of Chinese Paintings. Was employed by "Wen Hui Daily" and the "Youth Daily" as a journalist in fine arts.

1967 Went to Ye-Dang Mountain to paint the scenes.

1968 Traveled to Jinggang Mountain, Changsha, Xian, Tongchuan, Yean and into the Sichuan Province. Traveled to The Three Gorges as well.

1978 Traveled to Gueizhou and the Yunan Highland. Was particularly impressed by the scenes of the Big and Small Liang Mountains.

1980 Held "Eight People Painting Exhibition" in the People's Park in Shanghai.

1982 Traveled to Fuchuen River. Went passed by the Dayu Tomb and Lanting.

1983 Traveled again to Yedang Mountain.

1984 "Sunset and the Old Friend", portrait of Lipo, won the first-class prize of the National "poetry and painting" contest. This masterpiece was specially introduced by the "Books and Paintings" magazine.

1985 Traveled to the North-Western part of China. Visited the tombs of Ching emperors, Huo Qubing and other emperors. Observed the art of stone sculptures.

1986 Was introduced in the special report of "Chinese Paintings", commented by Mr. Ke Wenhui.
Traveled to Maiji Mountain for the art of stone sculptures. Traveled to Lanzhou and the Bingling Temple. Traveled to Zhangyi, Wuwei, Jiouchuen to Dunhuang. Traveled through the Qilien Mountain and the Erbao Prairie and entered Xining. Visited Taer Temple. Traveled to Lushan.

1987 Went to Xining again and climbed up to Hwashan. Traveled up north to Datong to observe "Buddhas of the Cloud Hill". Went passed by Taiyuan. Visited Jin Temple and the Two Forests Temple (in Pingyao). Traveled to Loyang to observe the Longmen Grottoes.
The portrait "Bada Shanren" was collected in the Shanghai Yearbook of Fine Arts. Comics "Bada Shanren" was published by Shanghai People's Art Publishing House (上海人民美術出版社).

1988 The landscape painting "Scenes of the journey to the west" was selected to be exhibited in the Shanghai Youth joint exhibition of Chinese paintings.
Xiao was invited to exhibit his masterpieces in the exhibitions given by the Shanghai Museum of Fine Arts in France, Italy and Belgium.
The landscape painting "The empty grain of rice" was the finalist of the Beijing International Exhibition on Chinese Ink Paintings.
Xiao's article "In search of the land of happiness" was published on the "Journal of Fine Arts". He also published the work he painted during the trip to the west.
Xiao was introduced by the special report of "Clouds" magazine.
Went to Huang-Shan to paint the scenes there.
Xiao was awarded the title of the "Master of Chinese Art Craftsmanship and Fine Arts" by the Department of Light Industries of the State Council of the People's Republic of China.

1989 Xiao published his landscape paintings and portraits in the "Clouds" magazine.
Xiao was invited to participate in the "Exhibition on the landscapes of the southern China" held at the Clouds Hall in Shanghai.
Xiao was invited by the Shanghai Academy of Chinese Paintings to give an exhibition of his work of art.

1990 Xiao published his landscape paintings in a special report of "The Artist" journal of Hong Kong. He was commented by Mr. Zhuang Yiling.
Xiao's landscape paintings were introduced by the special report of "The World of Chinese Cultures and Cultural Artifacts" of Hong Kong. He was commented by Mr. Yang Nianyue.
The book "Exhibitions of Xiao Haichun" was published by Da Ye publishing company.
Xiao was selected as the cover figure of "Talent" magazine.

1991 Xiao participated in the joint exhibition given by the "Three Stone Hall" in Hong Kong (with other painters such as Zhang Ding, Long Rui, Chen Xiangxun, Chen Ping, Zhao Wei and Lu Yushun).
Xiao participated in the joint exhibition given by the Shanghai Museum of Fine Arts (the other 3 painters are Chen Xinmao, Chu Ming and Wang Tiande).
Xiao was introduced by the special report of "Shanghai Huabao" (上海畫報). His work of art was commented by Mr. Liao Lu and collected in the Shanghai Yearbook of Fine Arts.
Xiao was invited to give a special interview to Shanghai XinMin Evening Daily.
Xiao participated in the first "Joint Exhibition on Chinese Landscape Paintings" given by the Research Institute of Chinese Paintings (中國畫研究院).

1993 Xiao participated in the "Shanghai-Taipei Chinese Ink Paintings Exhibition" given by Shanghai Museum of Fine Arts and other museums.
Xiao's profile was included in the "Profiles of the 100 Famous People of Chinese Paintings" edited by the Research Institute of Chinese Arts.
Xiao's work was collected in the "Collection of Paintings of Famous Painters from Shanghai" (Shanghai People's Art Publishing House).
Xiao, as a representative of Shanghai's landscape paintings, wrote a special report for the "Gallery" magazine. The article, entitled "A process with difficulties" talked about his creation of landscape paintings.
Xiao's work "The air of the early spring" won the awards of the "most excellent painting" and the "best painting for collection" in the second national exhibition of landscape paintings.

1994 Xiao gave an exhibition in the Dunhuang Art Center in Taipei.
Xiao gave an exhibition in "Zhuang Yishu" in Singapore.

1995 The Hanart Gallery held an exhibition for Xiao in the Hong Kong Arts Center. The exhibition was opened by Mr. T. T. Tsui, the famous businessman in Hong Kong.
Xiao participated in the "Exhibition of 15 Shanghai Painters" given by the Clouds Hall in Shanghai Museum of Fine Arts. The title of the exhibited painting is "Moonlight on the pond of lilies" (6 fans, 60X240cmX6).
Xiao's landscape paintings were introduced in "Chiangsu Journal of Paintings", issue February, 1995.
Xiao was invited by the Shanghai Museum of Fine Arts to give an exhibition on the modern Chinese paintings in Osaka, Japan.
Traveled to Yedang and Fuchun in autumn.

1996 Xiao participated in the Chinese New Year exhibition given by the Research Institute of Chinese paintings.
Xiao painted "The Red Dragonfly" (flowers and birds on 10 fans, 60X240cmX10).
Xiao painted "The 100 Children" (flowers on 6 fans, 60X240cmX6).
Xiao was invited by the Shanghai Museum of Fine Arts to give an exhibition on the modern Chinese paintings in France.
Xiao was invited by the Shanghai Museum of Fine Arts to give an exhibition on the modern Chinese paintings in Germany.
Xiao participated in the exhibition "A love affair with Jingang: Exhibition of landscape paintings of famous painters", co-organized by the Association of Chinese Artists and the Research Institute of Chinese Paintings, with his landscape paintings: "Jingang Mountain" (95X178cm), "Chusha Pass"(95X178cm).
Xiao was interviewed by the "Poetry and Paintings" program of Shanghai Television Station.
Xiao was invited to join trips to Malaysia and Singapore. The "Exhibition of Xiao Haichun's paintings" was given by the Dunhuang Art Company of Malaysia in the Royal Garden Hotel in Kuala Lumpur. The guests present at the opening reception included the deputy ministry of the post and telecommunication ministry of Malaysia and the Chinese ambassador to Malaysia. Xiao was also invited to give an interview to Radio Television Malaysia.
Xiao participated in the exhibition of modern Chinese ink paintings co-organized by the Clouds Hall and Liencheng Antique Store. His work "the Fortune-Calling Tree" was selected as the painting of the poster of this exhibition.

1997 Xiao went to Singapore to participate in the exhibition "Tradition and Innovation - Selected work of Xiao Haichun", given by the Cape of Goodhope Gallery in Singapore.
Xiao was invited by the Shanghai Museum of Fine Arts to give an exhibition on the modern Chinese paintings in Russia.
Xiao participated in "Great Exhibition of Chinese Arts - a celebration to the return of sovereignty of Hong Kong to the People's Republic of China", given by the Ministry of Culture of the PRC.
Xiao participated in the '97 Shanghai Arts Expo.
Xiao's work "The Dragon Mountain" (100X210cm) and "the Poetics of Mo-Jie" (100X210cm) were exhibited in the 35th Anniversary Exhibition of the Shanghai Academy of Chinese Paintings.
Xiao published the deluxe version of the calendar "A re-creation of the landscape - collections of landscape paintings by Xiao Haichun".
The oversized artbook of the "Collection of the 20th Century Chinese Ink Paintings - Xiao Haichun" was published by the Daye Company of Hong Kong, with prefaces written by Shao Dazhen, Chu Naizheng, Lu Fusheng and Hsu Jianrong.

1998 Xiao's work "The Division of Dawn and Dusk by Ying and Yang" (420X356cm) was selected as one of the paintings for the "Exhibition of 5000 years of civilization - the modern era", held in Guggenheim in 1998.

Xiao's painting "A Secluded Residence" was included in the "Exhibition of Contemporary Chinese Landscape and Oil Paintings of the International Year of Chinese Arts, 1998".
"The Red Dragonfly" was exhibited in the "Exhibition of 100 Quality Products of Shanghai".
Xiao participated in the first Shanghai biennial exhibition of Chinese paintings.
Went to Huang Shan to paint the scenes.
Trips to France, Luxemburg, the Netherlands, Belgium, Germany, Austria, Italy and Switzerland.

1999 Xiao edited the book of "ink and landscape paintings" of the collection of "the new concepts of the art of contemporary ink paintings". The chief editor of the collection was Gu Wuxuan.
Went to Huang Shan to paint the scenes.

2000 Xiao participated in the "Exhibition of New Chinese Paintings", organized by Lee Xiaoshan.
Xiao's work was selected and included in the oversized artbook of the "Contemporary Chinese Arts (the Chinese Paintings)".
Xiao's work was categorized in the book of landscape paintings of the "Guide to the contemporary arts" (Hubei).
Xiao participated in the "Exhibition of Contemporary Oil and Chinese Paintings" held in Finland by the Beijing Association of Oil Paintings.

2001 Xiao participated the "Exhibition of Chinese paintings in the past 100 years" held by the Chinese Association of Fine Arts.
Xiao participated in the first biennial exhibition of the National Academy of Paintings.
Xiao participated in every annual exhibition given by the Shanghai Academy of Chinese Paintings.
Xiao's work was selected to participate in the "2001 Shanghai Exhibition of Fine Arts".
Went to Huang Shan with students to paint the scenes.

2002 Xiao participated in the "Exhibition for the exchanges of the art of calligraphy between China and Japan".
Xiao was introduced by the focus reports of "Books and Paintings" of Shanghai (reported and photographed by Wu Lingtian, a self-written journal of art).
Went up to Huang Shan again in the rain with family.

2003 A series of articles by Xiao were published on a regular basis by "Books and Paintings" of Shanghai.
The "Xiao Haichun Ink Painting Studio" of the Liu Haisu Museum of Fine Arts was founded.
Xiao participated in the biennial exhibition of the National Academy of Paintings.
Xiao participated in the annual exhibition given by the Shanghai Academy of Chinese Paintings.
Xiao was nominated as one of the members of the examination and evaluation committee of the Shanghai exhibition of the arts of the young artists.
Went to Huang Shan with students to paint the scenes.

2004 The "Special Exhibition of Chinese Paintings of Xiao Haichun" will be held in the National Museum of History in Taipei in September.
A special collection of articles by Xiao Haichun will be published by Shanghai's Shu Hua Publishing House

國家圖書館出版品預行編目資料

名家水墨 ： 蕭海春 = Masterpieces of ink painting ： Xiao Haichun / 國立歷史博物館編輯委員會編輯. -- 初版. -- 臺北市 : 史博館, 民93
面 ； 公分
中英對照
ISBN 957-01-7989-9(精裝)

1. 水墨畫 - 作品集

945.6　　930140381

名家水墨：黃秋園、蕭海春作品聯展

展期：九十三年八月廿日至九月十二日
地點：國立歷史博物館 台北市南海路四十九號

主辦：國立歷史博物館
財團法人金鼎文教基金會
協辦：長流美術館
中華文化經濟協會

感謝各界給予本次展覽協助
金鼎文教基金會
張平沼先生

長流美術館
黃承志先生

敦煌藝術中心
洪平濤先生

名家水墨：蕭海春

發行人：黃永川
出版者：國立歷史博物館
台北市南海路四十九號
電話：886-2-23610270
傳真：886-2-23610171
網址：http: //www.nmh.gov.tw
編輯：國立歷史博物館編輯委員會
主輯：戈思明
執行編輯：謝世英
助理編輯：王慧珍
美術設計：陳光輝 眞澄製作
攝影：張冠豪
翻譯：謝世英 萬象翻譯社
英文審稿：邱勢淙
印刷：士鳳藝術設計印刷有限公司
出版日期：中華民國九十三年八月初版
定價：新台幣1200元
展售處：國立歷史博物館文化服務處
統一編號：1009302519
ISBN：957-01-7989-9（精裝）

Masterpieces of Ink painting: A Joint Exhibition of Works by Huang Qiuyuan & Xiao Haichun

Dates: Aug. 20-Sep. 12, 2004
Venue: National Museum of History, 49, Nan-hai Road, Taipei, Taiwan

Catalogue: Masterpieces of Ink Painting: Xiao Haichun

Publisher: HUANG Yung-chuan
National Museum of History
49, Nan-hai Road, Taipei, Taiwan
Tel: 886-2-23610270
Fax: 886-2-23706031
http://www.nmh.gov.tw
Editor: Editorial Committee of National Museum of History
Editor in Chief: Jeff GE
Curatorial Editor: HSIEH Shih-ying
Executive Editors: HSIEH Shih-ying, WANG Hui-jen
Photographer: Zhang Guanhao
Designed by Michael K.H. CHEN
Translator: HSIEH Shih-ying, Elite Translators
Proofreader: Mark ROWSON
Printing by Shih Fong Art Printing Co., Ltd.
Publishing Date: Aug. 2004
Price: NT$ 1200
Gift Shop: Cultural Service Department of National Museum of History
GPN:1009302519
I S B N:957-01-7989-9-(Hard cover)

FIRST EDITION